Torah Treasures

Torah Treasures

Selected Thoughts and Insights from
the Classic Commentaries on the
Parshah of the Week

Compiled and Annotated by
DOV FURER

BERAISHIS
SHEMOS

בראשית
שמות

Copyright © 1987

Published by C.I.S. Publications
a division of C.I.S. Communications Inc.
674 Eighth Street, Lakewood, N.J. 08701
(201) 367-7858/364-1629

Published in conjunction with
STAM Gemilas Chessed Fund Publications
of Lakewood, New Jersey

ISBN 0-935063-24-2 h/c
ISBN 0-935063-25-0 s/c

All rights reserved. This book, or any part thereof, may not be reproduced in any form whatsoever without the express written permission of the publisher.

Cover design by Ronda Kruger Green
Book design by Devora Oberman
Book production by Chaya Hoberman and Shami Reinman

Printed by Gross Bros., Union City, New Jersey

Dedication

"תפארת בנים אבותם"

This sefer is lovingly dedicated
to the memory
of our
Husband, Father and Grandfather

יוסף בן משה אקערמאן ז"ל
Mr. Joseph Ackerman
of blessed memory

A man who came to these shores
after enduring the bitter hardships
of Poland and Siberia
with the single-minded determination
to rebuild his family
with total dedication to Torah and Mitzvos.
May his example inspire us
to continue in the path he set forth
and may he be a מליץ יושר for all the משפחה.

Mrs. Pearl Ackerman
Mr. and Mrs. Eliezer Furer and Family
Dr. and Mrs. Jacob Ackerman and Family
Mrs. Ruth Kram and Family

מכתב ברכה

RABBI ABRAHAM PAM
582 EAST SEVENTH STREET
BROOKLYN, NEW YORK, N. Y.
11218

בס"ד

חי"י טבת, תשמ"ז

ראיתי את החבור Torah Treasures, לקט אמרים ורעיונות מרבותינו גדולי הדורות ומאורי ישראל מסודרים על פרשיות השבוע ומתורגמים בשפת המדינה לתועלת הרבים, שלוקט ואסף ביגיעה רבה ובטוב טעם ודעת תלמיד ותיק בבית מדרשנו במתיבתא תורה ודעת הי"ה ר' דוב פורער שליט"א.

הנה ד"ת ומוסר המופיעים בחבור זה, הנובעים ממעיינות התורה שחפרום גדולי עולם, אינם צריכים חיזוק והסכמה, ואך למותר להכביר מלים בשבחם.

והנני רק לברך את מע"כ המחבר שליט"א שיזכה להמשיך לשבת באהלה של תורה, ולעטר תורתנו הקדושה בעטורי סופרים, ולהפיץ פרי עמלו לזכות את הרבים ולהרבות כבוד שמים בעולם.

בכבוד ויקר,

אברהם יעקב הכהן פאם

Acknowledgments

The purpose of this *sefer* is to present a broad and varied collection of enlightening and thought-provoking comments on the weekly *Parshah* in an accessible English-language format. The reader will find selections from classic Torah commentators ranging from penetrating insights into the basic meanings to intriguing perspectives such as *gematriyaos*, whereby new meanings for words and phrases are found by analyzing the numerical values of their letters. With sources such as the Vilna Gaon, Chida, *Chasam Sofer* and *Bais Halevi*, this *sefer* should prove convenient and useful for all those who do not have access to the Hebrew originals.

If the *sefer* will serve to enhance the *Shabbos* tables of its readers, stimulating lively discussion among families, if it will serve to introduce new thoughts, greater knowledge and a more profound Torah consciousness among its readers, then the objectives of the author will have been met.

This *sefer* is lovingly dedicated to the memory of my grandfather Mr. Joseph Ackerman ז״ל, an individual whose outstanding and tenacious dedication to the *chinuch* of his children was a beacon of light in an era of darkness. May this *sefer* be an eternal *zchus* for his *neshamah*, and may we also merit that my grandmother Mrs. Pearl Ackerman שתחי׳ לאוי״ט continue to inspire us for many years with the qualities they jointly imparted to us in the past.

I would like to take this opportunity to thank my brother-in-law Rabbi Avraham Peker for initially conceiving the concept of this work and my uncle Dr. Jacob Ackerman whose constant encouragement and support brought the project from an idea to fruition.

I also owe a debt of gratitude to my brother-in-law Rabbi Dovid Elias, Rosh Kollel of Kollel Keser Torah in Montreal, and to Rabbi Pinchus Gershon Waxman, a wonderful friend, both of whom gave constantly of their time and effort throughout the project, providing suggestions and advice through every stage of the work. I am also deeply indebted to Yeshivah Torah Vodaath for providing me with a warm environment of ד' אמות של הלכה.

This *sefer* is very much the product of the professional skills of Reb Avraham Yaakov Finkel, who translated the manuscript into its present eminently readable English form. My thanks are extended to him for his excellent work. A special note of thanks is also due the editorial and graphics departments of C.I.S. Communications of Lakewood, New Jersey, for their highly original book and cover design and for their exemplary efforts in the entire production process of this *sefer*.

To my dear parents Mr. and Mrs. Eliezer Furer I owe an immeasurable debt of gratitude for their selfless devotion to my every need מעודי ועד היום הזה. May the *Ribono Shel Olam* grant them many long and happy years, with מנוחת הנפש and הרחבת הדעת. May they merit only *nachas* and joy from their children and grandchildren.

Most of all, I humbly thank the *Ribono Shel Olam* for giving me the ability and the opportunity to labor in His Torah. May I be deemed worthy of His continued סייעתא דשמיא for all the years to come.

Dov Furer
Chanukah 5747

Table of Contents

Beraishis בראשית

Beraishis	17	בראשית
Noach	27	נח
Lech Lecha	33	לך לך
Vayeira	45	וירא
Chayai Sarah	57	חיי שרה
Toldos	65	תולדות
Vayaitzai	75	ויצא
Vayishlach	83	וישלח
Vayaishev	89	וישב
Mikaytz	97	מקץ
Vayigash	109	ויגש
Vayechi	119	ויחי

Shemos שמות

Shemos	129	שמות
Vo'aira	137	וארא
Bo	143	בא
Beshalach	151	בשלח
Yisro	167	יתרו
Mishpatim	177	משפטים
Terumah	191	תרומה
Tetzaveh	203	תצוה
Ki Sissa	211	כי תשא
Vayakheil	223	ויקהל
Pikudei	231	פקודי

Torah Treasures

Beraishis / בראשית

Beraishis / בראשית

בראשית ברא אלקים...
In the beginning the Lord created...

Hashem used a ב, *bais*, which has a numerical value of 2, rather than an א, *aleph*, as the opening letter of the Torah, because He intended it to serve as an allusion to the two worlds He created, this world and the World to Come. It was also meant to hint at the two essential parts of Torah, the Written Law and the Oral Law, because the world was created in the merit of Torah and those who study its holy words.

Baal Haturim

בראשית ברא אלקים...
In the beginning the Lord created...

The Vilna Gaon states that all the 613 commandments can be traced to the word בראשית, *beraishis*. The question was put to him: "If this be true, then where in the word *beraishis* can you show us a clue to the commandment of פדיון הבן, *pidyon haben*, the redemption of the

[א:א] בראשית ברא אלקים את השמים ואת הארץ.

[1:1] In the beginning the Lord created the heavens and the earth.

TORAH TREASURES • *Beraishis*

firstborn son after thirty days?"

Without hesitating, the Vilna Gaon replied, "The word בראשית forms the acrostic of the first letters of the following sentence: בן ראשון אחר שלשים יום תפדה which translates to: Redeem your firstborn son after thirty days."

Vilna Gaon

[א:א] בראשית ברא אלקים את השמים ואת הארץ.

[1:1] **In the beginning the Lord created the heavens and the earth.**

בראשית ברא אלקים . . .
In the beginning the Lord created . . .

Rabbi Yitzchak introduces his comments in *Beraishis Rabba* with a quote from *Tehillim* 119:160: ראש דברך אמת, *the beginning of Your Word is truth*. This may be taken in its literal sense, for the acrostic of the last letters of the first three words of the Torah בראשית ברא אלקים form the word אמת, *truth*. Thus, the beginning of Hashem's Word—the Torah—is indeed truth.

This interpretation also offers an interesting solution to the age-old question of why the Torah begins with the letter ב, *bais*, rather than with the letter א, *aleph*.

Before attempting to answer this question, however, let us take a brief look at the function of גימטריא, *gematria*, the numerical value of Hebrew words, and מספר קטן, *mispar katan*, the contraction of these numerical values.

Generally, the full values of the letters of a Hebrew word are added to each other to determine the numerical value, resulting in the *gematria* of that word. When the system of *mispar katan* is used, numerical values are determined by adding the digits of the full value to each other. For instance, the numerical value of 12, when employing *mispar katan*, would become 1 + 2 = 3; the number 35 would

18

בראשית • TORAH TREASURES

become 3 + 5 = 8; 50 would become 5 + 0 = 5.

Based on *mispar katan* computation, the word אמת would result in a value of 9, as follows: א = 1, מ = 40 and 4 + 0 = 4; ת = 400, and 4 + 0 + 0 = 4. Thus, 1 + 4 + 4 = 9.

Mathematically, the number 9 has special significance. If we begin counting with the number 2, we will note that the sum of each grouping of three successive digits (e.g. 2-3-4, 5-6-7, 8-9-10, etc.) totals 9 in *mispar katan*. Note the results of the addition: 2 + 3 + 4 = 9; 5 + 6 + 7 = 18 and 1 + 8 = 9; 8 + 9 + 10 = 27 and 2 + 7 = 9. Ad infinitum, the outcome will always be 9, the equivalent of truth.

Now, if we follow the same *mispar katan* calculation, starting with א, *aleph*, (e.g. 1-2-3, 4-5-6, 7-8-9, etc.) the result is different. Once again, we arrive at a constant, but this time the number is 6. Note the results of the addition: 1 + 2 + 3 = 6; 4 + 5 + 6 = 15 and 1 + 5 = 6; 7 + 8 + 9 = 24 and 2 + 4 = 6.

Surprisingly, the number 6 is the numerical equivalent in *mispar katan* of the word שקר, *falsehood*, as follows: ש = 300 and 3 + 0 + 0 = 3; ק = 100 and 1 + 0 + 0 = 1; ר = 200 and 2 + 0 + 0 = 2. Thus, 3 + 1 + 2 = 6.

Thus we may conclude that rather than opening the Torah with *aleph*, with its numerical connotations of שקר, Hashem began the Torah with the letter *bais*, numerically alluding to the inherent truth of the Torah.

Dorshei Reshumos

והארץ היתה תהו ובהו . . .
And the earth was formless and desolate . . .

The *Midrash* tells us that when the world was first created, Hashem desired the deeds of the righteous and the deeds of the wicked.

[א:ב-ד] והארץ היתה תהו ובהו וחשך על פני תהום ורוח אלקים מרחפת על פני המים. ויאמר אלקים יהי אור ויהי אור. וירא אלקים

TORAH TREASURES • *Beraishis*

את האור כי טוב ויבדל אלקים בין האור ובין החשך.

[1:2-4] **And the earth was formless and desolate, with darkness upon the face of the abyss, and the spirit of the Lord swept across the water. And the Lord said; "Let there be light," and there was light. And the Lord saw that the light was good, and the Lord divided the light from the darkness.**

"And the earth was formless and desolate" refers to the deeds of the wicked. "And the Lord said 'Let there be light,' " refers to the deeds of the righteous. Still, how would we know whose deeds He preferred? When it is written, "And the Lord saw that the light was good," it becomes clear that He desires the deeds of the righteous and not the deeds of the wicked.

The words of the *Midrash* are seemingly incomprehensible. It is inconceivable that Hashem has any desire for the deeds of the wicked, let alone that He should prefer them over the deeds of the righteous.

The answer can be found in the saying of our Sages that just as the Name of Hashem is sanctified by rewards to the worthy, it is also sanctified by the punishment meted out to the wicked. This then in the meaning of the *Midrash*. Hashem desires to punish the wicked and to reward the righteous, because both of these bring honor to his Name. Which of the two methods does He prefer? When the Torah tells us that Hashem saw that "the light was good," we learn that He prefers to enhance His Honor by rewarding the righteous.

Binyan Ariel

[א:יא] ויאמר אלקים תדשא הארץ דשא עשב מזריע זרע עץ פרי עשה פרי למינו אשר זרעו בו על הארץ ויהי כן.

[1:11] **And the Lord said: "Let the earth put forth grass; vegetation yielding seed, and fruit trees bearing fruit of its own**

ויאמר אלקים תדשא הארץ דשא . . .
And the Lord said: Let the earth put forth grass . . .

The *Mishnah* in *Avos* 1:18 teaches a fundamental lesson: Rabban Shimon ben Gamliel tells us that the world endures because of three things—justice, truth and peace, as it is written: "Truth and the judgment of peace are you to judge in your gates." (*Zechariah* 8:16)

The word דשא, *grass*, in the aforementioned verse in *Beraishis* forms an acrostic which corroborates Rabban Shimon ben Gamliel's statement. The letters ד־ש־א are the initials of the three pillars of the world he enumerates: דין, *justice*, שלום, *peace*, and אמת, *truth*.

Hashem's command may thus be read as follows: "Let the earth put forth דשא (grass), i.e. דין, שלום and אמת (justice, peace, and truth) in order that it will endure.

Baal Halevushim

ויאמר אלקים נעשה אדם . . .
And the Lord said: Let us make man . . .

Rabbi Shimon said: "When Hashem proposed to create man, the Attribute of Kindness said, 'Let man be created, for he bestows kindness.'

"The Attribute of Truth said, 'Let man not be created, since he is inherently a liar.'

"The Attribute of Righteousness said, 'Let man be created, for he does acts of righteousness.'

"The Attribute of Peace said, 'Let him not be created, since he is quarrelsome and contentious.'

"How did Hashem resolve this dilemma? He took hold of Truth and hurled it to earth."

In other words, Hashem rejected the advice of the Attribute of Truth.

Now, the obvious question arises: What benefit did Hashem gain by disposing of Truth when Peace, which also opposed man's creation, still occupied its influential position?

We can solve this problem by noting that Kindness and Righteousness, who were in favor of man's creation, would now constitute a 2-1 majority against Peace, and so the decision was made to create man.

But still we may ask, why was Truth hurled

---

kind that contains its own seed shall be upon the earth." And it was so.

[א:כו] ויאמר אלקים נעשה אדם בצלמנו כדמותנו וירדו בדגת הים ובעוף השמים ובבהמה ובכל הארץ ובכל הרמש הרמש על הארץ.

[1:26] And the Lord said: "Let us make man in Our Image, after Our Likeness, and let them have dominion over the fish of the sea, the birds of the sky and the cattle, and over all the earth, and over every creature that creeps upon the earth."

TORAH TREASURES • *Beraishis*

to earth rather than Peace. After all, both of them opposed man's creation with equal vigor? The answer is that Truth cannot be defeated or outvoted by any majority; it is invincible, unshakable, never to be overwhelmed by numbers.

Mekoroseinu Ha'attikim

[א:לא-ב:א] וירא אלקים את כל אשר עשה והנה טוב מאד ויהי ערב ויהי בקר יום הששי. ויכלו השמים והארץ וכל צבאם.

[1:31-2:1] **And the Lord saw everything He had made, and behold, it was very good; and there was evening and there was morning, the sixth day. And the heavens and the earth and all their hosts were completed.**

וירא אלקים את כל אשר עשה . . .
And the Lord saw everything he had made . . .

The recitation of the *Kiddush* on *Shabbos* begins with the words יום הששי, *the sixth day*, followed by ויכלו השמים, *and the heavens and the earth were completed*. We combine the two sentences, even though in the Torah they are not at all connected. "The sixth day" is a phrase that comes at the end of verse 1:31, forming the completion of that chapter, whereas "and the heavens and the earth were completed" is the opening verse of the next chapter (2:1).

Nonetheless, we do follow this practice, the reason being that the first letters of יום הששי, in conjunction with the first letters of ויכלו השמים, form the acrostic of Hashem's Holy Name שם הוי"ה (the Tetragrammaton).

We follow the custom of reciting in a low voice the words preceding "the sixth day," namely ויהי ערב ויהי בקר, *and there was evening and there was morning*. We do this in order to keep the words "the sixth day" unfragmented within their Scriptural context.

Others begin the *Kiddush* at the start of verse 31, "And the Lord saw everything He had made, and behold, it was very good." They do this based on the rabbinic injunction not to divide a verse, unless it was so divided by Moshe Rabbeinu.

Otzar Chaim

[ב:כא] ויפל ה׳ אלקים תרדמה על האדם ויישן ויקח אחת מצלעתיו ויסגר בשר תחתנה.

[2:21] And Hashem the Lord caused a deep sleep to fall upon the man, and he slept; and He took one of his ribs and closed up the place with flesh.

ויפל . . .
And Hashem the Lord caused to fall . . .

The following admonition is ascribed to Rabbi Eliezer Gordon of Telz: From the choice of the word ויפל, *and he caused to fall*, with regard to sleep, we may deduce that sleep has a connotation of downfall and ruin. This is certainly true, for when asleep one is not conscious and has no awareness of life. Therefore, curtail your sleep and make every effort to stay awake and alert.

Memayanos Hanetzach

Author's Note:
On this same subject, Rabbi Chaim Schmulevitz זצ״ל related that Napoleon would exert himself to stay awake in order not to be deprived of even one moment of the sweet taste of being emperor.

[ב:כב] ויבן ה׳ אלקים את הצלע אשר לקח מן האדם לאשה ויבאה אל האדם.

[2:22] And Hashem the Lord constructed the rib He had taken from the man into a woman, and He brought her to the man.

הצלע . . .
. . . the rib

The Hebrew word for the rib is הצלע. By rearranging these letters, the word לעצה, *to the counsel*, emerges. What is the significance of this transposition? The meaning becomes clear when we examine the *Gemara* in *Bava Metzia* (59a) which states: "Though your wife may be of diminutive stature, yield to her and follow her advice."

In other words, a husband is to listen לעצה, *to the counsel*, of his wife (who was formed from the rib).

Chida

[ג:יא] ויאמר מי הגיד לך כי עירם אתה המן העץ אשר צויתיך לבלתי אכל ממנו אכלת.

ויאמר מי הגיד . . .
And He said: "Who told you . . ."

The *Gemara* (*Chulin* 139a) sees the word

[3:11] And he said: "Who told you that you are naked? Have you eaten from the tree from which I have forbidden you to eat?"

המן, *can it be that from,* in this verse as an allusion to המן, *Haman,* which has an identical spelling.

The question arises: Is the connection between Haman and this verse merely in a coincidental spelling or is there a more profound connection?

Upon reflection, there is a very real parallel. Haman had all a person could possibly want—wealth, status, power. Yet, he was not satisfied so long as Mordechai would not bow down to him. He had to have absolutely everything! Adam Harishon also had all he could ask for. He lived in Gan Eden and lacked nothing. Yet, he could not resist tasting the fruits of the *Eitz Hadaas,* the Tree of Knowledge. He had to have everything!

Traditional

[ג:יד] ויאמר ה׳ אלקים אל הנחש כי עשית זאת ארור אתה מכל הבהמה ומכל חית השדה על גחנך תלך ועפר תאכל כל ימי חייך.

[3:14] And Hashem the Lord said to the serpent: "Because you have done this, you are cursed from among all cattle, and from all the beasts of the field; upon your belly shall you go, and dust shall you eat all the days of your life."

... ועפר תאכל כל ימי חייך

... and dust shall you eat all the days of your life

At first glance, this does not appear to be a curse. In fact, it might even be considered a blessing. Inasmuch as the serpent will only eat dust, it will never lack for food, since it will always find an abundance of nourishment.

But therein lies its curse. Concerning the other creatures of the world, it is written, "He gives the beast his food, and to the young ravens which cry." (*Tehillim* 147:9) The serpent, however, surrounded as he is by an inexhaustible supply of his sustenance, never has the need to turn to Hashem in prayer, asking Him to provide for it. Thus, in effect, the serpent was banished from Hashem's Presence.

It is as though Hashem had said: "I have provided for all your needs, so that you will never have to approach me again."

Likutei Basar Likutei

בראשית • TORAH TREASURES

ויקרא האדם שם אשתו חוה כי היא היתה אם כל חי
And Adam named his wife Chavah, because she was the mother of all living

According to some commentaries, this took place after Chavah caused Adam to sin. If so, there is an important lesson to be learned here.

In these circumstances, after Chavah had caused a decree of death to be issued against Adam and all his future generations, he did not react by divorcing her and driving her away. On the contrary, he focused on the good within her, on the fact that she would be the ancestress of all future generations. And even after she brought death into the world, he gave her a name which commemorated her bond of life. Regarding himself, however, Adam did not choose a new name, but kept his original name of Adam, which denotes his origin from *adamah*, the lowly soil.

In this, Adam taught us an invaluable lesson. He was humble and aware of his own shortcomings, but he saw only the good in others.

Oznaim Latorah

[3:20] And Adam named his wife Chavah, because she was the mother of all living.

ויאמר קין אל הבל אחיו . . .
And Kayin spoke to his brother Hevel . . .

The verse does not mention what it was that Kayin said to Hevel. However, an explanation to this verse can be derived from the *Midrash* which tells us that Hevel was exceedingly strong, far stronger than Kayin. It follows, therefore, that Kayin could not possibly have overcome Hevel in a direct confrontation. His only chance of success was through subterfuge and treachery. He put on a friendly face and spoke to Hevel in a way that lulled him

[4:8] And Kayin spoke to his brother Hevel, and it came to pass when they were in the field that Kayin rose up against his brother Hevel and he killed him.

into a false sense of security. Then he killed him.

This then is the meaning of the verse. "And Kayin spoke to his brother Hevel," meaning, he spoke to Hevel with false brotherliness. Because of this, Hevel had no suspicions, and "when they were in the field that Kayin . . . killed him."

Vilna Gaon

[ונח מצא חן בעיני ה' [ו:ח]

[6:8] **And Noach found favor in the eyes of Hashem.**

ונח מצא חן בעיני ה'
And Noach found favor in the eyes of Hashem

The words ונח, *and Noach,* may allude to the following saying in *Pirkei Avos* 3:13: "Whoever is pleasing to his fellows is also pleasing to the Omnipresent." The word נח is used here to connote "is pleasing."

The Torah states that נח found favor in the eyes of Hashem. Consequently, this verse can be expounded as follows: If one conducts himself in the נח spirit, i.e. he acts virtuously towards his fellow man, then he will find favor in the eyes of Hashem.

Sefer Chassidim writes in a similar vein: "And Noach found favor." Whoever is נח, *calm,* and controls his anger, finds חן, *favor,* and is well-liked.

Noting that the noun נח has the connotation of quiet, rest or tranquility, it may be said that Noach's character is implied in his name.

Likewise, we may say that the name Noach predestined him for the חן, *favor,* that was bestowed on him, for by invertng the letters נח, the word חן is obtained.

Chida

Noach / נח

. . . את האלקים התהלך נח
. . . Noach walked with the Lord

The commentary *Netzach Yisrael* expounds the three words האלקים התהלך נח stating, "If you form a word, using the last letters of these three words in their reverse order the result is חכם, *sage*. This indicates that Noach was a wise man."

It is written, "Wisdom is a stronghold to the wise man". (*Koheles* 7:19) This is homiletically interpreted as referring to Noach, who was indeed a venerable Sage.

Furthermore, our Rabbis state that Noach studied the Torah. They find an allusion to this in the Scriptural phrase, ויבן נח, *and Noach built. (Beraishis* 7:20) In a different context, this phrase might also be translated as *"and Noach understood."* (The verbs בנה, *to build*, and בין, *to understand*, are closely related.)

Thus, ויבן נח may be rendered as *"he understood"* his Torah studies; he carefully weighed and considered the different aspects of each

---

[ט:ו] אלה תולדת נח נח איש צדיק תמים היה בדרתיו את האלקים התהלך נח.

[6:9] These are the chronicles of Noach. Noach was a righteous and wholehearted man in his generations; Noach walked with the Lord.

TORAH TREASURES • *Noach*

[ו:ט] אלה תולדת נח נח איש צדיק תמים היה בדרתיו את האלקים התהלך נח.

[6:9] **These are the chronicles of Noach. Noach was a righteous and wholehearted man in his generations; Noach walked with the Lord.**

question, and he was deliberate in his judgment.

The fact that only the reverse arrangement of the letters produces the word חכם demonstrates that Noach was not an ordinary wise man. He was a great Sage, who contemplated each proposition from both its positive and negative aspects, as thesis and antithesis. He studied each question forward and backward, and he did this because he did not trust his intuition to arrive at the truth.

Concerning Noach the Torah states, "A whole-hearted man was he in his generation." Rashi (*Avodah Zarah* 6a) defines the meaning of תמים, *whole-hearted*, as the quality of humility and meekness. Thus, it may be said that Noach was a humble man, and it was this quality of meekness that prompted him to analyze each problem so thoroughly, considering all aspects and viewing it from all angles.

In his sincere modesty, he did not believe he had the ability to arrive at the truth in a flash of intuitive genius. He searched for truth through the long and arduous process of reasoning, in the manner of a true Sage, and thus he arrived at the Truth of Torah.

The well-known Talmudic rule that the opinions of Bais Hillel are always authoritative (*Eruvin* 6b) is predicated on a similar idea. Because the scholars of Bais Hillel possessed humility, as the *Gemara* notes, "Always let a person be humble like Hillel", (*Shabbos* 30b) their view is considered authoritative. For a humble person, not confident of his wisdom, will dissect, scrutinize and sift through each problem until a clear solution emerges and he arrives at the truth.

Chida

נח • TORAH TREASURES

ויראאלקים את הארץ והנה נשחתה כי השחית כל בשר את דרכו על הארץ
And the Lord saw the earth, and behold, it was corrupt, for all flesh had corrupted its way upon the earth.

The apparent redundancy in the duplication of the word "corrupt" offers a revealing insight. Without the Torah, moral and ethical values are determined not by Hashem's law, but by the mores of contemporary society. When immorality is the accepted norm, then it ceases to be a vice, and depravity becomes the life-style of that society.

Viewing our verse in this light, a new meaning emerges.

"And the Lord saw the earth, and behold, it was corrupt." In other words, it was corrupt only in the eyes of the Lord. Why? "For all flesh had corrupted its way upon the earth." In other words, the people of that generation were not aware of their own depravity; immorality was their way of life.

Har Tzvi

[ו:יא-יב] ותשחת הארץ לפני האלקים ותמלא הארץ חמס. וירא אלקים את הארץ והנה נשחתה כי השחית כל בשר את דרכו על הארץ.

[6:11-12] And the earth was corrupt before the Lord, and the earth was filled with violence. And the Lord saw the earth, and behold, it was corrupt, for all flesh had corrupted its way upon the earth.

צהר תעשה לתבה . . .
Make a skylight for the ark . . .

Rashi brings two views as to the meaning of the word צהר. One translates it as a skylight, the other as a glittering jewel which provided the תבה with illumination. Rashi also brings two views on an earlier verse (6:9) "Noach was a righteous and wholehearted man in his generation." One view sees this as a complimentary statement, that even in a corrupt generation, he was a righteous man; the other view sees it as a derogatory statement, that only in a corrupt generation such as his could he be considered a righteous man. It can be

[ו:טז] צהר תעשה לתבה ואל אמה תכלנה מלמעלה ופתח התבה בצדה תשים תחתים שנים ושלשים תעשה.

[6:16] "Make a skylight for the ark, and taper it to a cubit at the top, and place the door of the ark in its side, make a lower, second and third level for it."

TORAH TREASURES • *Noach*

said that these two sets of views are interrelated.

Rashi, in explaining another verse (19:17), tells us that if a person is rescued from a calamity through no merit of his own, he has no right to observe the destruction of the others left behind. Thus, Lot and his wife, who were rescued from Sedom through the merit of Avraham, were not permitted to turn around and observe the destruction of Sedom.

Similarly, at the time of the flood, if Noach was truly a righteous man then he would be allowed a skylight through which he could observe the destruction of the corrupt people. However, if Noach was not truly a righteous man, he could not be allowed a skylight through which he could observe the effects of the flood, and the illumination within the ark had to come from a glittering jewel.

Pardes Yosef

[כא: ו] ואתה קח לך מכל מאכל אשר יאכל ואספת אליך והיה לך ולהם לאכלה.

[6:21] **And you, take for yourself all the food that may be eaten, and gather it to you, and it shall be food for you and for them.**

ואתה קח לך מכל מאכל אשר יאכל . . .
And you, take for yourself all the food that may be eaten . . .

Two questions present themselves. First, the words "that may be eaten" seem to be superfluous. Furthermore, is it conceivable that Noach stored a quantity of food sufficient to feed the animals in the ark for an entire year?

For an answer to both questions we must turn to a statement by our Sages. They interpret the verse "all the food that may be eaten" (*Vayikra* 11:34) as applying to the amount of food that can be eaten in one gulp. The Rabbis calculate (*Yoma* 80a) that the maximum the human throat can swallow at one time is a quantity the size of an egg.

At any rate, it is apparent that the words אשר יאכל, *that may be eaten,* refer to the amount of food that can be eaten in one swallow.

We can now explain the verse as follows: "And you take for yourself all the food that may be eaten," meaning, take one mouthful for each meal. Hashem will bestow his blessing on the food so that it will satiate you.

"And it shall be food for you and for them"; even though you will only eat no more than a mouthful, nevertheless each one will be satisfied.
Vilna Gaon

שנים שנים באו אל נח . . .
Two by two they came to Noach. . .

[7:9] שנים שנים באו אל נח אל התבה זכר ונקבה כאשר צוה אלקים את נח.

[7:9] **Two by two they came to Noach into the ark, male and female, as the Lord had commanded Noach.**

The *Midrash* tells us that this verse refers to those days on which the entire *Hallel* is recited. Rabbi Shimshon of Ostropoli offers the following ingenious solution to this enigmatic *Midrash*:

The word בבטח is the *siman*, the means of remembering, those days on which the entire *Hallel* is recited outside of Eretz Yisrael. ב equals 2, referring to the first two days of *Pesach;* ב equals 2, referring to both days of *Shavuos;* ט equals 9, referring to the nine days of *Succos;* ח equals 8, referring to the eight days of *Chanukah.*

The *Midrash* wants to tell us that the very same idea is concealed in this verse. שנים means 2, referring to the first two days of *Pesach;* שנים means 2, referring to both days of *Shavuos;* באו has a numerical value of 9, referring to the nine days of *Sukkos;* אל נח has a numerical value of 89, which is the equivalent of חנוכה, *Chanukah,* whose *gematria* is also 89.

TORAH TREASURES • *Noach*

Thus, the verse does indeed allude to all the days on which the entire *Hallel* is recited.

Likutei Besamim

[ח:יד] ובחדש השני בשבעה ועשרים יום לחדש יבשה הארץ.

[8:14] **And in the second month, on the twenty-seventh day of the month, the earth became dry.**

...יבשה הארץ
... the earth became dry

The numerical value of יבשה הארץ, *the earth became dry*, amounts to 613. The lesson to be learned from this is that in the merit of the 613 commandments which Yisrael was destined to receive in the future, the earth became dry.

Netzach Yisrael

[יא:א] ויהי כל הארץ שפה אחת ודברים אחדים.

[12:1] **And the whole earth was of one language, and of one kind of words.**

...שפה אחת
One language ...

Rashi explains the words "one language" to mean לשון הקדש, *the holy tongue*. It is significant to note that שפה אחת and לשון הקדש have the same numerical value, which would corroborate Rashi's statement.

Rabbeinu Eliezer of Worms

Author's note:

The two numerical values are not exactly equal. The *gematria* of שפה אחת equals 794, whereas that of לשון הקדש amounts to 795. It is one of the basic rules of *gematria*, that two values may be considered equal even though there is a difference of one between them.

Lech Lecha / לך לך

לך לך...
Go away...

The numerical value of לך לך, *go away*, is 100.

By the choice of these words, Hashem wished to indicate to Avram that when he would reach one hundred years of age, the blessing "I will make of you a great nation" would be fulfilled, for when Avram was one hundred years old his son Yitzchak was born.

Also, by using these words, Hashem wanted to hint to Avram that after leaving his country he would live one hundred more years. He was seventy-five years old when he left, and he lived for one hundred and seventy-five years.

Baal Haturim

[יב:א-ב] ויאמר ה' אל אברם לך לך מארצך וממולדתך ומבית אביך אל הארץ אשר אראך. ואעשך לגוי גדול ואברכך ואגדלה שמך והיה ברכה.

[12:1-2] And Hashem said to Avram: "Go away from your land, and from your birthplace and from your father's house, to the land that I will show you. And I will make of you a great nation, and I will bless you and make your name great; and you shall be a blessing."

לך לך...
Go away...

Rashi explains that with the word לך, Hashem made the implied promise to Avram that his departure from his homeland would

TORAH TREASURES • *Lech Lecha*

be "for your pleasure and your benefit."

To preface the next question it should be noted that Hashem's command to "Go away from your land" constituted one of the ten trials with which He tested Avram's faith.

We are now faced with an apparent inconsistency. If, as Rashi states, Hashem gave the assurance that Avram would incur no harm as a result of his leaving, that he would actually derive great benefit from it, how then could his obedience be considered a test of his faith?

The answer may be found in a subsequent verse (12:4): "So Avram went as Hashem had spoken to him." These words state unequivocally that Avram's one and only motive for leaving was his wish to fulfill Hashem's command.

He was tested to ascertain the true motive for leaving his homeland. Knowing that richness and fame were in store for him, would Avram leave with the intention of claiming the promised reward, or would he do so for the purely spiritual purpose of obeying Hashem's command?

Hafla'ah

[יב:א] ויאמר ה' אל אברם לך לך מארצך וממולדתך ומבית אביך אל הארץ אשר אראך.

[12:1] **And Hashem said to Avram: "Go away from your land, and from your birthplace and from your father's house, to the land that I will show you.**

לך לך מארצך וממולדתך ומבית אביך . . .
Go away from your land, and from your birthplace and from your father's house . . .

We are struck by the unusual order of events as they are arranged in this passage. One would say that a person who leaves his country first departs from his father's house, then from his birthplace, and finally, he leaves his homeland.

The following then, should have been the order in which the verse should have listed them: "Go away from your father's house, from your birthplace, and from your land."

We must understand, however, that Avram was commanded to take leave of Ur Kasdim, not only by physically removing himself, but also in a spiritual sense. He was to distance himself from the society in which he had grown up, to completely forget and erase from his consciousness any trace of his native land, his birthplace, his father's house, and the pagan culture they represented.

When it comes to eradicating ingrained impressions and habits, those which were formed in early childhood in the home environment are the most deeply rooted ones and survive the longest.

Indeed, the order of priority in the verse is quite appropriate. Avram would first forget his land, then his birthplace and only much, much later his father's house, his parents and his family.

Alshich

ואעשך לגוי גדול . . .
And I will make of you a great nation. . .

The *Gemara* (*Pesachim* 17a) expounds this verse:

"I will make of you a great nation" alludes to the fact that we say in our prayer "Hashem of Avraham."

"And I will bless you" alludes to the fact that we say "Hashem of Yitzchak."

"I will make your name great" alludes to the fact that we say "Hashem of Yaakov."

The simple meaning of "I will make your name great" is that your name אברם, *Avram*, will be changed to אברהם, *Avraham*. This interpretation can be reconciled with the

[יב:ב] ואעשך לגוי גדול ואברכך ואגדלה שמך והיה ברכה.

[12:2] "And I will make of you a great nation, and I will bless you and make your name great; and you shall be a blessing."

TORAH TREASURES • *Lech Lecha*

[יב:ב] ואעשך לגוי גדול ואברכך ואגדלה שמך והיה ברכה.

[12:2] "And I will make of you a great nation, and I will bless you and make your name great; and you shall be a blessing."

homiletic interpretation "Hashem of Yaakov" if we consider the following:

It is interesting to note that the names of the *Avos*, אברהם, יצחק and יעקב, are composed of a total of 13 letters, which correspond to the 13 Divine attributes of mercy.

Your name will be made great and you will be called Avraham because we say Hashem of Yaakov. If, however, we would say Hashem of Yisrael (another name for Yaakov), then your name would have to remain Avram, if the total of 13 letters is to be maintained, since אברם, יצחק, ישראל have 13 letters. But now that we say Hashem of Yaakov, it becomes necessary to lengthen the name אברם to אברהם in order to reach the sum of 13 letters.

This then is the meaning of what the *Gemara* tells us. "I will make of you a great nation" alludes to the fact that we say in our prayer "Hashem of Avraham."

An alternate explanation may be found in the following approach:

Yaakov was given the name Yisrael, because Hashem wanted to include in it the divine name א-ל.

Thus the statement "I will make your name great because we say Hashem of Yaakov" is understood as follows: If we would say Hashem of Yisrael we would cast aspersions on Avraham and belittle him by implying that he did not merit to have א-ל incorporated in his name.

I will make your name great because we say Hashem of Yaakov teaches us that Avraham's name became great by the fact that we associate Hashem with Yaakov who is his offspring. Had we said "Hashem of Yisrael," a name which includes א-ל, it could be taken as

36

a sign of disrespect towards Avraham.

Chomas Anoch

ואברכה מברכיך ומקללך אאר . . .
And I will bless those that bless you, and those that curse you I will curse . . .

The two parts of this verse present a contrast. In the first part, the predicate is followed by the object, whereas in the second part the object precedes the predicate.

Kli Yakar, noting this contrast, offers an illuminating insight. Good intentions, though not yet carried out, are rewarded by Hashem as accomplished deeds. Evil intentions, on the other hand, are punishable only when they have been put into effect.

Therefore, the Torah states "I will bless them" at the beginning of the verse in order to indicate that they will be blessed from the moment they intend to bless you; even though they have not actually done so as yet. The opposite is true of "those that curse you." Here bad intentions do not count as deeds. Therefore, "I will curse" follows after "and those that curse you."

Kli Yakar

[12:3] "And I will bless those that bless you, and those that curse you I will curse, and all the families of the earth shall want to be blessed like you."

ולא נשא אתם הארץ לשבת יחדו . . .
And the land was not able to bear them. . .

Rabbi Meir Simcha Hakohain raises the question: Why does the Torah repeat the statement "that they could not dwell together?" He bases his response on the foibles of human nature.

Every quarrel is triggered by a dispute. When the argument erupts, both parties fight for what they perceive as their rightful posi-

[13:6] And the land was not able to bear them, that they might dwell together, for their wealth was great, and they could not dwell together.

TORAH TREASURES • *Lech Lecha*

tion. As the conflict expands and the flames of hatred and passion engulf the battleground, the fight for justice becomes a fight for the sake of quarreling. They tear at each other, attack, slur and defame each other, without knowing the reason for the dispute, without remembering the cause that gave rise to it; truly *sin'as chinam,* hostility without a cause.

Thus, the verse begins, "And the land was not able to bear them, that they might dwell together," the reason being "for their wealth was great." But in the end it came to the point that "they could not dwell together," for no reason at all, without knowing the why and wherefore.

Rabbi Meir Simcha Hakohain

[יג:טז] ושמתי את זרעך כעפר הארץ אשר אם יוכל איש למנות את עפר הארץ גם זרעך ימנה.

[13:16] **And I will make your offspring like the dust of the earth, that if a man could count the dust of the earth, then your seed will also be counted.**

... גם זרעך ימנה

... then your seed will also be counted

The last letters of these three words form the word מכה, *plague,* alluding to the plague that is to follow in the wake of any counting of the children of Israel, as did in fact occur in the days of David Hamelech. (*Shmuel II* 21:1)

Chomas Anoch

[טו:ח] ויאמר אדני אלקים במה אדע כי אירשנה.

[15:8] **And he said: "O my Master, O Lord, how can I know that I shall inherit it?"**

ויאמר אדני ...

And he said: "O my Master ..."

The *Gemara* (*Berachos* 7b) tells us that Rabbi Yochanan said in the name of Rabbi Shimon ben Yochai: Since the day that Hashem created the universe, no one had called Hashem by the name אדון, *master,* until Avraham came and called him אדון, in the above verse.

The author of the responsa *Kanfei Yonah,* in the introduction to his work, relates that someone once asked the Vilna Gaon for a letter of approbation (*haskamah*) for his commentary on the siddur. The Vilna Gaon read the opening pages and found an explanation as to why the order of the morning prayers begin with the hymn to Hashem's glory, אדון עולם, *Adon Olam*. The exposition, based on the above-mentioned statement by Rabbi Shimon ben Yochai read as follows: "Since we know that Avraham initiated the morning prayer service it is proper and fitting that this service be opened with the divine appellation *Adon*, which he was the first to use."

The Vilna Gaon exclaimed that the publication of this siddur would be worthwhile if only for this one commentary.

Iturei Torah

. . . כי גר יהיה זרעך בארץ לא להם
. . . that your offspring shall be a stranger in a land that is not theirs

[טו:יג] ויאמר לאברם ידע תדע כי גר יהיה זרעך בארץ לא להם ועבדום וענו אתם ארבע מאות שנה.

[15:13] **And He said to Avram: "Be assured that your offspring shall be a stranger in a land that is not theirs, and they shall enslave them, and they shall afflict them four hundred years."**

Our Sages (*Chullin* 60b) explain the verse "He moved the people to cities" (*Beraishis* 47:21) to mean that Yosef relocated the Egyptians from one city to another in order to remind them that henceforth they had no claim of ownership to the land. His intention was to remove from his brothers the stigma of foreigner, since every Egyptian, by Yosef's decree, now had become an exile.

With this in mind, the abovementioned verse can be viewed in a new light. "Be assured that your offspring shall be a stranger," but do not think that their banishment will be a source of disgrace. Certainly not. For they will be exiled to "a land that is not theirs," referring to the Egyptians. In other words, the land of your children's exile will not belong to

TORAH TREASURES • *Lech Lecha*

the Egyptians who live there. They will not be able to scorn your children by calling them exiles, for Yosef will have transferred every Egyptian from his birthplace to another city.

This also explains the apparent redundancy of the words "shall be a stranger" and "in a land that is not theirs," for if the latter clause refers to the Egyptian people, there is then no duplication in the text.

Arizal

The verse in *Shemos* 22:20 can be explained in a similar vein. "And a stranger you shall not wrong, neither shall you oppress him, for you were strangers in the land of Egypt." Hashem is telling us, "Do not wrong him by calling him a stranger. Observe what I have done for you. I banished you to a land where the inhabitants themselves were strangers, in order to save you from shame. Therefore, you too shall not wrong a stranger."

Nachal Kedumim

[יז:ד-ה] אני הנה בריתי אתך והיית לאב המון גוים. ולא יקרא עוד את שמך אברם והיה שמך אברהם כי אב המון גוים נתתיך.

[17:4-5] "As for Me, behold, My covenant is with you, and you shall be the father of a multitude of nations. And your name shall no longer be Avram, but your name shall be Avraham, for I have made you the father of a multitude of nations."

... אני הנה בריתי אתך

As for me, behold, My covenant is with you ...

The juxtaposition of these two verses, one dealing with covenant, the other one dealing with name, provides a source for the custom of giving the name at the time of the *bris milah* (circumcision).

Commentaries

... המול לכם כל זכר

... circumcise every male among you

The Rabbis teach that Avraham performed all the *mitzvos* of the Torah even though the

Torah had not yet been given. Why then did he fulfill the *mitzvah* of *milah* only after Hashem actually commanded it? A possible answer to this question is suggested by the term *bris milah*, which means the covenant of circumcision.

Every covenant or contract requires two participants. In the case of *bris milah*, the two parties were Hashem and Avraham. Before Hashem promulgated the covenant of *milah*, Avraham was the only partner, and with one partner there can be no *bris*, no covenant, no *mitzvah* of *milah*. Thus, for Avraham to perform the *milah* on his own accord would not have constituted the fulfillment of a *mitzvah*.

Rabbi Yitzchak Zev Soloveitchik

[יז:י] זאת בריתי אשר תשמרו ביני וביניכם ובין זרעך אחריך המול לכם כל זכר.

[17:10] "This is my covenant which you shall keep between Me and you and your offspring after you: circumcise every male among you."

המול לכם כל זכר . . .
. . . circumcise every male among you

The fact that Avraham fulfilled the *mitzvah* of *milah* only after receiving Hashem's command, while he performed all other *mitzvos* on his own accord may be predicated on the rabbinic dictum: "One who acts in compliance with a command is superior to one who acts voluntarily." While Avraham performed all *mitzvos* on his own accord, he fully intended to fulfill them again after Hashem would proclaim them in the Torah, and thus earn the higher degree of merit. With the *mitzvah* of *milah*, however, this approach was impossible, since this *mitzvah* can be performed only one time.

Avodas Israel

TORAH TREASURES • *Lech Lecha*

[יז:כו] בעצם היום הזה
נמול אברהם וישמעאל
בנו.

[17:26] In the middle of that very day, Avraham and his son Yishmael were circumcised.

בעצם היום הזה נמול . . .
In the middle of that very day . . .

Avraham fulfilled the *mitzvah* of *milah* on Yom Kippur, and indeed, the numerical value of the words בעצם היום הזה נמול equals that of the words יום הכפורים. Therefore, in the merit of his doing the *mitzvah*, on this day each year the blood of Avraham's *milah* becomes manifest before Hashem as the blood of sacrifices and helps atone for the sins of Klal Yisrael of the entire year.

Likewise, we find that the chapter that relates the story of Avraham's *milah* contains a total of 356 words, which is equal to the *gematria* of the word כפורים. This is another allusion to Avraham's *milah* atoning for Klal Yisrael's sins of the entire year.

Nachal Kedumim

Author's note:

The aforementioned *gematria* will only yield the desired result if the word נמול is spelled in its complete form, including the letter י, *yud*, whereas in the Torah text it is spelled in its abbreviated form, without a *yud*. Nevertheless, we may say that in the case of this *gematria*, we follow the pronunciation. Since the word נמול is vocalized as though it were spelled with a *yud* we count the *yud* in the letters of the *gematria*.

Avudraham is quoted in *Nachal Kedumim*, *Yisro*, as stating that the numerical value of the words ה' מלך, ה' מלך, ה' ימלוך לעולם ועד (Hashem reigns, Hashem reigned, Hashem will reign) equals the *gematria* of כתר, *crown*, namely 620. However, in the Torah text, where the latter part of the sentence is mentioned (*Shemos* 15:18) both the words ימלך and לעלם

are written without a ו, *vav*. Consequently, lacking the two letters *vav*, the total value is 12 less than כתר. Here too, we are compelled, for the sake of the *gematria*, to adhere to the phonetic transcription, rather than to the Scriptural text. (This thought is also expressed by Mizrachi, *Bamdibar* 15:39.)

As to בעצם היום הזה נמול adding up to 416 and יום הכפורים to 417, this discrepancy does not present a problem. It is one of the basic rules of *gematria* that two values may be considered equal even though there is a numerical difference of one between them.

וכל אנשי ביתו ...
And all the men of his household ...

Rabbi Zvi Elimelech of Dinov, in his *Igra d'Pirka*, quotes Rabbi Shlomo of Karlin, stating:

It says in the *Midrash* that when Hashem directed Eliyahu to make his appearance at every *bris*, he addressed Hashem and said:

"Hashem, O Hashem, you know I am jealous for the sake of Your great Name. Now, in the event that the father of the child should be a sinner, how will I be able to endure his presence?"

Hashem promised him to grant forgiveness to the child's father.

"But what if the *Mohel* is a transgressor?" Eliyahu continued.

Hashem promised to forgive the sins of the *Mohel*.

But Eliyahu persisted, "What if there are transgressors among the invited guests?"

Hashem promised to grant atonement to the entire assemblage.

Memayanos Hanetzach

[יז:כז] וכל אנשי ביתו יליד בית ומקנת כסף מאת בן נכר נמלו אתו.

[17:27] And all the men of his household, those born in the house, and those bought with money from a foreigner, were circumcised with him.

Vayeira / וירא

... והנה שלשה אנשים נצבים עליו
... and behold, three men stood before him

In the weekly portion of *Vayeira*, we learn of the hospitality practiced by Avraham and subsequently by Lot.

Concerning Avraham the text reads: "And when he saw them, he ran to meet them." The same was said of Lot when he met the angels (19:1), "And Lot saw them and rose up to meet them." Thus, we may ask, wherein lies the difference between Avraham's hospitality and Lot's?

With regard to Avraham the verse states, "And behold, three men stood beside him." The inference is that Avraham perceived his visitors as ordinary men; in fact, as Rashi explains, he considered them to be idolatrous Arabs. And yet, "when he saw them, he ran to meet them." By contrast, regarding Lot it says, "And the two angels came to Lot at evening." Should Lot be commended for offering hospitality to angels? After all, who would not want to welcome angels into his home!?

Bais Halevi

[יח:ב] וישא עיניו וירא והנה שלשה אנשים נצבים עליו וירץ לקראתם מפתח האהל וישתחו ארצה.

[18:2] **And he lifted up his eyes and looked, and behold, three men stood before him, and when he saw them, he ran to meet them from the entrance of the tent, and he bowed down to the earth.**

Vayeira

... והנה שלשה
and behold, three ...

The numerical value of והנה שלשה, *and behold, three*, equals the numerical value of אלו מיכאל גבריאל ורפאל, *these were Michael, Gavriel, and Raphael*. According to *Midrash Rabba*, these were the very three angels who visited Avraham.

Chomas Anoch

... אל נא תעבר מעל עבדך
... Pass not away, I pray, from your servant

[יח:ג] ויאמר אדני אם נא מצאתי חן בעיניך אל נא תעבר מעל עבדך.

[18:3] And he said: "My Lord, if now I have found favor in your sight, pass not away, I pray, from your servant.

The *Gemara* in *Shabbos* 127a explains that this verse teaches us that the practice of hospitality takes precedence over receiving the Divine Presence, as it is written, "He said, 'My Lord, if now I have found favor with You, pass not away ...'" According to the *Gemara's* interpretation, Avraham was addressing Hashem, asking him to wait until after he had welcomed the guests into his home.

How are we to apply this lesson to our every day lives?

The Baal Shem Tov observes, "Our Sages teach us an important lesson. Even though the practice of hospitality sometimes involves neglect of Torah study or having to listen to innocent gossip, things which are anathema to the Divine Presence, it still takes first priority."

Otzar Chaim

ואקחה פת לחם ...
And I will fetch a morsel of bread ...

[יח:ה] ואקחה פת לחם וסעדו לבכם אחר תעברו כי על כן עברתם על עבדכם ויאמרו כן תעשה כאשר דברת.

[18:5] And I will fetch

This verse alludes to the practice that the head of the household breaks the bread.

Baal Haturim

Author's note:
The head of the household breaks the bread, even if a *Kohein* or a *Talmid Chacham* is seated at the table, the reason being that he will break it into generous portions. A guest, the bread not being his own, will hand out smaller pieces.

[יח:ו] וימהר אברהם האהלה אל שרה ויאמר מהרי שלש סאים קמח סלת לושי ועשי עגות.

[18:6] And Avraham hastened into the tent to Sarah, and said: "Make ready quickly three measures of fine meal, knead it, and make cakes."

a morsel of bread, and satiate your heart, after that you shall pass on; inasmuch as you have come to your servant. And they said: "So do, as you have said."

... לושי ועשי עגות
... knead it and make cakes

Why did Avraham find it necessary to instruct Sarah to "knead it"? Surely, Sarah must have known how to prepare cakes. We would have expected Avraham merely to say, "Make cakes."

An answer suggests itself when we consider our Rabbi's contention that this episode occurred on *Pesach*. The Torah prohibits any work to be done on a festival with the exception of the preparation of food for human consumption. Thus kneading, baking, slaughtering and cooking are permitted. Any work before kneading, such as grinding the wheat etc. is forbidden.

Consequently, by telling her to "knead it," Avraham indicated to Sarah that only work required from the point of kneading was permitted.

Traditional

למועד אשוב אליך ...
At the set time I will return to you ...

The word למועד, *at the set time*, provides an allusion in support of the statement of *Chazal* that Yitzchak was born on *Pesach*. The numerical value of this word is equivalent to the numerical value of בפסח, *on Pesach*. At the set

[יח:יד] היפלא מה' דבר למועד אשוב אליך כעת חי' ולשרה בן.

[18:14] "Is anything too hard for Hashem? At the set time I will return to you, when the season comes round, and Sarah shall have a son."

TORAH TREASURES • *Vayeira*

time, which is *Pesach*, Yitzchak will be born.

Daas Zekeinim Mibaalei Hatosefos

[יח:טז] ויקמו משם האנשים וישקפו על פני סדם ואברהם הלך עמם לשלחם.

[18:16] **And the men rose up from there and looked out toward Sedom, and Avraham went with them to direct them on their way.**

[יח:יט] כי ידעתיו למען אשר יצוה את בניו ואת ביתו אחריו ושמרו דרך ה' לעשות צדקה ומשפט למען הביא ה' על אברהם את אשר דבר עליו.

[18:19] **For I have known him so that he may command his children and his household after him that they keep the way of Hashem, to do righteousness and justice,**

ויקמו משם האנשים וישקפו על פני סדם ...
And the men rose up from there and looked out toward Sedom ...

At first glance, the word משם, *from there*, appears superfluous within the context of this passage. However, upon reflection, a deeper meaning of the word emerges.

When the angels compared Avraham's intense piety and generous hospitality to the wickedness and depravity of the people of Sedom, their anger and sense of outrage rose to new heights.

Accordingly, we can interpret the verse as follows: "And the men rose up *from there*," from Avraham's house, which was permeated with holiness, purity, righteousness and benevolence. "From there," from their experiences in Avraham's house, they derived reinforcement for their determination to destroy Sedom.

Therefore, וישקפו על פני סדם, *and they looked out toward Sedom*. The term used for "and they looked out" is וישקפו, in consonance with the rabbinic rule כל השקפה לרעה, that השקפה denotes looking out that bodes ill, with ominous overtones. Since they had just come from Avraham's house, their "look" at Sedom showed clearly that it had to be destroyed.

Kli Chemdah

... אשר יצוה את בניו
... that he may command his children

The word formed by the last letters of these words is תורה, *Torah*. Torah is the teaching to

48

be transmitted to his children.
Baal Haturim

אולי יש חמשים צדיקם בתוך העיר ...
Perhaps there are fifty righteous men in the midst of the city ...

The emphasis is on the words בתוך העיר, *in the midst of the city.* Avraham did not ask for compassion for the sake of fifty righteous men who just happened to dwell in the city. Rather, his prayer was for fifty righteous men who live in the midst of the city. A righteous man in the midst of Sedom's depravity is not one who withdraws into his own cocoon thinking that he has done quite enough if he saves himself and at most his household. The righteous man for whose sake Avraham prayed that the entire city be saved is to be found in the midst of the city, actively involved in the lives of all its inhabitants. He never ceases to admonish, teach, warn, rebuke and save souls, wherever and however he can. He never despairs and never tires of trying, however distant the hopes of success may be.
Rabbi Shamson Raphael Hirsch

אולי יש חמשים צדיקם בתוך העיר ...
Perhaps there be fifty righteous men in the midst of the city ...

Rabbi Yochanan said: "Wherever the word צדיקם, *righteous men*, is mentioned in connection with Sedom, it is written without the second י, *yud*, to indicate that they were not perfectly righteous." (*Beraishis Rabba* 4a)

Meshech Chochmah explains (also mentioned in the Collected Writings of *Sfas Emes*), that the verse places stress on בתוך העיר, *in the*

TORAH TREASURES • *Vayeira*

midst of the city, in order to imply that even though they would not be considered righteous men in another city, nevertheless, compared to the people of this city they were virtuous indeed; therefore, do not destroy the place for their sake.

This corresponds to the above mentioned *Midrash*, which states that the righteous men of Sedom were not righteous in every respect.

Yalkut Yehudah

[כא:כה-כו] והוכח אברהם את אבימלך על אדות באר המים אשר גזלו עבדי אבימלך. ויאמר אבימלך לא ידעתי מי עשה את הדבר הזה וגם אתה לא הגדת לי וגם אנכי לא שמעתי בלתי היום.

[21:25-26] And Avraham reproved Avimelech because of the well of water which Avimelech's servants had stolen. And Avimelech said: "I know not who has done this thing; neither did you tell me, nor have I heard of it before today."

ויאמר אבימלך לא ידעתי מי עשה את הדבר הזה . . .

And Avimelech said: "I know not who has done this thing..."

For what reason does the Torah relate that before Avraham established the covenant he admonished Avimelech and that Avimelech apologized saying that he was unaware of his servants' thievery?

The answer can be found in the ruling which prohibits the making of a covenant with a descendant of Noach who does not observe all of the seven Noachide Commandments. Noting that Avimelech's servants were guilty of robbery and that they had not been brought to justice, both violations of Noachide laws, Avraham objected to entering a covenant with Avimelech. Avimelech, in turn, offered as an excuse, "I know not who has done this thing."

Rabbi Chaim Soloveitchik of Brisk

[כא:לג] ויטע אשל בבאר שבע ויקרא שם בשם ה' א-ל עולם.

[21:33] And he planted a tamarisk tree in Be'er Sheva, and called there on the name

ויטע אשל בבאר שבע . . .

And he planted a tamarisk tree in Be'er Sheva...

אשל, *tamarisk tree*, is the acronym formed of the first letters of אכילה, *eating*, שתיה, *drinking*, לינה, *lodging*. By planting an אשל, Avraham may have wished to hint at his

50

ויראTORAH TREASURES

intention to repair the damage brought about by Adam through eating, by Noach through drinking, and by Lot, amongst the people of Sedom, through lodging.

of Hashem, the Lord of the Universe.

Vilna Gaon

Author's note:
The original text of the Vilna Gaon's writings show an alternate reading: לויה, *escort*, instead of לינה, *lodging*.

ויהי אחר הדברים האלה והאלקים נסה את אברהם ...
And it came to pass after these things that the Lord tested Avraham...

"After these things" refers to the words of Satan, as recounted in *Gemara Sanhedrin* 89b:

Concerning Yitzchak it is written, "And the child grew and he was weaned, and Avraham made a feast." (Beraishis 21:8)

Satan said to Hashem: "Master of the Universe! You granted this old man a child at one hundred years of age. Yet, though he made a sumptuous feast he could not find one single turtledove or young pigeon to offer to you."

Hashem replied: "He did it all for his son. If I were to command him to sacrifice his son for Me, he would do so without hesitation."

Thereafter, "Hashem tested Avraham."

The *Gemara's* exposition still leaves Satan's question unanswered. Since Avraham had prepared this lavish feast for his guests, why indeed, did he not also offer at least one sacrifice to Hashem?

The truth is that there was no need for a specific sacrifice, inasmuch as the entire feast, being a *seudas mitzvah*, a feast celebrating the performance of a mitzvah, was an offering to Hashem. We know that Avraham's bound-

[כב:א] ויהי אחר הדברים האלה והאלקים נסה את אברהם ויאמר אליו אברהם ויאמר הנני.

[22:1] And it came to pass after these things that the Lord tested Avraham and said to him: "Avraham!" And he said: "Here I am."

less joy at the birth of his son was attributable solely to the fact that having a son enabled him to instruct this child in the service of Hashem, as it is written, "So that he will command his children and his household." (18:19).

The entire meal was, therefore, a *seudas mitzvah*. But Satan imputed unholy motives to Avraham, saying, "He could not find one single turtledove or young pigeon to offer to you."

Whereupon, Hashem replied: "If I would command him to sacrifice his son for Me, he would do so without hesitation, for he derives all his joy from worshipping Hashem, and indeed, the entire feast in an expression of gratitude to Me."

Ksav Sofer

[כב:ה] ויאמר אברהם אל נעריו שבו לכם פה עם החמור ואני והנער נלכה עד כה ונשתחוה ונשובה אליכם.

[22:5] **And Avraham said to his lads: "Stay here with the donkey, and I and the lad will go yonder and prostrate ourselves and come back to you."**

... ואני והנער נלכה עד כה ונשתחוה ונשובה אליכם

... and I and the lad will go yonder and prostrate ourselves and come back to you

Their need to prostrate themselves seems unclear. In order to discover the significance of these words we turn to *Devarim* 26:10, where the Torah describes the bringing of the *bikkurim*, the first fruits. We read there: "You shall set it down (the basket) before Hashem your Lord and prostrate yourself before Hashem your Lord." *Aderes Eliyahu* offers the following commentary: "And prostrate yourself" is a general rule that one is to prostrate himself upon leaving the *Bais Hamikdash*. Thus, since Avraham and Yitzchak were at the site of the *Bais Hamikdash*, they were under the obligation to prostrate themselves.

Vay15   Rabbi Yitzchak Zev Soloveitchik

ויקרא אליו מלאך ה' מן השמים...
And an angel of Hashem called to him from heaven...

Who indeed was this angel? This angel was the very angel that was created through this *mitzvah*, the binding of Yitzchak. This is based on the teachings of Chazal that every *mitzvah* performed leads to the creation of an angel that serves as a divine agent to bring reward for this *mitzvah*. With this great *mitzvah* having now been completed in meticulous detail, an angel of Hashem had indeed been created. However, had Avraham actually sacrificed Yitzchak, it would have been considered an act of murder, since it was not the Will of Hashem that Yitzchak be sacrificed, only offered. Therefore, it was this very angel which prevented the deed that would have nullified his existence.

Accordingly, the *Midrash* states that the angels cried when Avraham wanted to sacrifice his son Yitzchak. These were the angels that were created from the many facets that the *Akeidah* involved, taking (*"take your son"*), going (*"go to the land of Moriah"*), erecting the altar (*"build the altar there"*), arranging the wood (*"he arranged the wood"*), binding (*"he bound his son Yitzchak"*), and bringing him up to the altar (*"he placed him on the altar on top of the wood"*), each individual *mitzvah* leading to the creation of an angel whose existence and survival derived from it. Had Avraham sacrificed Yitzchak, however, all these individual acts, in retrospect, would no longer have been *mitzvos* but preparations for murder. Therefore, these angels wept, for it would have meant their own extinction.

[כב:יא-יב] ויקרא אליו מלאך ה' מן השמים ויאמר אברהם אברהם ויאמר הנני. ויאמר אל תשלח ידך אל הנער ואל תעש לו מאומה כי עתה ידעתי כי ירא אלקים אתה ולא חשכת את בנך את יחידך ממני.

[22:11-12] And an angel of Hashem called to him from heaven and said: "Avraham, Avraham!" And he said: "Here I am." And he said: "Stretch not your hand towards the lad, nor do the slightest thing to him, for now do I know that you fear Hashem and did not withhold your son, your only son, from Me."

TORAH TREASURES • *Vayeira*

Now the meaning of the verse becomes clear. "For now do I know that you fear Hashem and did not withhold your son, your only son from Me." In other words, from the fact that I was created as a result of this *mitzvah* and from my continued existence, I know that you fear Hashem.

Malbim

[כב:יז] כי ברך
אברכך והרבה ארבה את
זרעך ככוכבי השמים
וכחול אשר על שפת הים
וירש זרעך את שער
איביו.

[22:17] **For I will assuredly bless you and multiply your offspring as the stars of the heavens and as the sand which is on the seashore; and your offspring shall inherit the gates of their enemies.**

... וירש זרעך את שער איביו

... And your offspring shall inherit the gates of their enemies

Cruelty is a deplorable character trait, in many ways comparable to a progressive disease. By committing one barbarous act of cruelty, one's entire personality becomes infected with this harmful characteristic.

At the *Akeidah*, Avraham had to make use of the quality of cruelty, but he did so for the greater glory of Hashem, for by this act of total self-nullification he proclaimed Hashem's supremacy in the world.

Having proved that even cruelty can be used in the service of Hashem, Avraham received Hashem's promise that his descendants would "inherit the gates of their enemies," meaning that they would be victorious in a war concerning which compassion was forbidden, as it is written, "You shall let live nothing that breathes." (*Devarim* 22:16)

One would think that this requires a great deal of ruthlessness. "Yet, I know," says Hashem, "through your offspring all the nations of the earth will bless themselves" (*Beraishis* 22:18) for they will recognize that your seeming savagery was not rooted in hardness of heart; rather, it was a manifesta-

54

tion of your fulfillment of Hashem's command.

Otzar Chaim

Author's note:
It should be noted that Pinchas, for his zealous act, was blessed by Hashem with a "covenant of peace" (*Bamidbar* 25:12), proving that his deed was not prompted by ruthlessness but by a pure and sincere desire to restore peace.

Chayai Sarah / חיי שרה

ויהיו חיי שרה ...
And the life of Sarah was ...

The numerical value of ויהיו is equal to 37. This *gematria* suggests that, in fact, Sarah lived only 37 years, that is to say, years in which she lived a full, rewarding life. This is because Yitzchak was born when she had reached 90 years of age, and she lived to be 127 years old. *Chazal* state that anyone who is childless is not considered alive. Thus, she did not derive any delight or joy from life until Yitzchak was born. Her remaining 37 years, however, were filled with happiness.

Al Hatorah

ויהיו חיי שרה מאה שנה ועשרים שנה ושבע שנים ...
And the life of Sarah was one hundred years and twenty years and seven years ...

This is the only place in the Torah where the age of a woman is recorded. The reason is that Sarah was the matriarch of the Jewish people, as it is written, "Look to Avraham your father,

[כג:א] ויהיו חיי שרה
מאה שנה ועשרים שנה
ושבע שנים שני חיי
שרה.

[23:1] And the life of Sarah was one hundred years and twenty years and seven years, these were the years of Sarah's life.

TORAH TREASURES • *Chayai-Sarah*

and to Sarah that bore you." (*Yeshayah 51:2*)

Sar 2   Zohar

[כג:טז] וישמע
אברהם אל עפרון וישקל
אברהם לעפרן את הכסף
אשר דבר באזני בני חת
ארבע מאות שקל כסף
עבר לסחר.

[23:16] **And Avraham listened to Efron, and Avraham weighed out for Efron the silver which he had named in the earshot of the sons of Ches, four hundred shekels of silver of mercantile currency.**

וישקל אברהם לעפרן את הכסף ...
And Avraham weighed out for Efron the silver ...

The name Efron occurs twice in this verse. The first time it is spelled *mallai*, in its full form, with a ו, *vav*; by contrast, the second time, in connection with the payment of 400 shekels, it is spelled *chaseir*, in the abbreviated form, without a *vav*.

Baal Haturim notes a significant *gematria*. Efron, in the abbreviated form, has a numerical value of 400, the exact amount he received as payment for the field of *Me'aras Hamachpelah*.

Baal Haturim

... עבר לסחר

... mercantile currency

The word סחר, *merchant*, contains an allusion to an important lesson in ethics.

The letters in the *aleph beis* which precede those in this word are נ, *nun*, (preceding ס, *samach*), ז, *zayin*, (preceding ח, *ches*), and ק, *kuf*, (preceding ר, *reish*). Together they yield the word נזק, *damage or injury*. The word עבר, *current*, also denotes priority or precedence, as in עבר לעשייתן (a term indicating that a *brachah* must be said prior to the performance of any *mitzvah*).

Based on this, עבר לסחר may be translated homiletically as "note the letters that precede סחר, which jointly produce נזק."

Let us now examine Efron's character as it is revealed in his dealings with Avraham. He was miserly and greedy, and as a result, he

58

חיי שרה • TORAH TREASURES

suffered damage, as our Sages expound the verse in *Mishlei* 28:22: "He that has an evil eye hastens after riches, and knows not that want shall come upon him." The word used for want in this verse is חסר which contains the same letters as סחר.

There is a fundamental lesson in business ethics conveyed in this. סחר, *conduct of commerce*, is linked to חסר, *loss*, and נזק, *damage*. There are numerous pitfalls a businessman must avoid, such as swindling, stealing, telling untruths and all manner of other wrongdoing. If he is vigilant in his practices, then his סחר, *his business*, will flourish, as he fulfills Hashem's Will. On the other hand, if he is ruthless and dishonest, then נזק, *damage*, and חסר, *loss*, will ensue.

Chomas Anoch

לאברהם למקנה לעיני בני חת . . .
To Avraham for a possession in the presence of the sons of Ches . . .

Why the particular stress on לעיני בני חת, *in the presence of the sons of Ches*? The *Meshech Chochmah* offers the following enlightening explanation:

The *Shulchan Aruch* (*Choshen Mishpat* 190) rules that land can be acquired by means of either payment (*kessef*), a deed (*shtar*), or a physical act of possession (*chazakah*).

However, according to Rav Hai Gaon, a Jew can acquire land from a non-Jew only by transfer of a deed or a physical act of possession (as cited in the commentary of the Vilna Gaon, note 194); he cannot establish ownership by payment only. Because of this, our Sages decreed that if a Jew buys a house from a non-Jew in Eretz Yisrael, a deed must be

[כג:יח] לאברהם
למקנה לעיני בני חת בכל
באי שער עירו.

[23:18] To Avraham for a possession in the presence of the sons of Ches, before all that went in at the gate of the city.

TORAH TREASURES • *Chayai-Sarah*

written (by the non-Jew), even on *Shabbos*, since such an acquisition can not be effected by payment.

Now it becomes clear why the emphasis is on לעיני בני חת, *in the presence of the sons of Ches.* These words, literally translated, mean in the eyes of the sons of Ches. In other words, by paying the 400 silver shekels he acquired the field only "in the eyes of the sons of Ches," according to their view, but according to Jewish law, he would acquire ownership to the field and the cave only through the physical act of possession of burying his wife Sarah there. Accordingly, we read in verse 20 that after the burial "the field and the cave were established to Avraham as an ancestral burial site by the sons of Ches." Only then was the legal acquisition accomplished.

Meshech Chochmah

[כד:ד] כי אל ארצי ואל מולדתי תלך ולקחת אשה לבני ליצחק.

[24:4] **But you shall go to my country and to my birthplace and take a wife for my son, for Yitzchak.**

... ולקחת אשה לבני ליצחק
... and take a wife for my son, for Yitzchak

Later in the text (24:38), when Eliezer relates the purpose of his mission to the city of Nachor, he says: "My master made me swear... take a wife for my son," pointedly omitting any mention of the name Yitzchak.

This omission can be explained with the help of a parable.

A wealthy man sought the son of a great Torah sage as a match for his marriageable daughter. To this end, he set aside for her a substantial dowry. A clever matchmaker suggested to him, "Since you are ready to spend such a huge sum of money for the son of a Torah great, I have for you a young suitor who is a Torah giant himself."

The rich man rejected the match, saying: "I

don't want my daughter to become a rabbi's wife. I don't want her to suffer hardships and be deprived of the pleasures of life."

Eliezer's story is analogous to this. Avraham told Eliezer, "Take a wife for my son, for Yitzchak." You are to point out that my son is a great *tzaddik* in his own right. Eliezer, however, noting the baseness of the people with whom he was dealing, feared that a suitor of such high caliber would be rejected. Therefore, he emphasized only the eminence and grandeur of the suitor's father, without making any mention of Yitzchak himself.

Bais Halevi

ואמר אל אדני אלי לא תלך האשה אחרי
And I said to my master: "Perhaps the woman will not wish to follow me"

Rashi explains: The word אלי, *perhaps*, appears in its abbreviated spelling, without a ו, *vav*, so that it can also be read אלי, *to me*. Eliezer had a daughter, and he was hoping "the woman will not wish to follow him" so that he could give his own daughter in marriage to Yitzchak.

It is interesting to note that when the Torah relates the story as it actually happened, Eliezer's words אולי לא תאבה האשה, *perhaps the woman will not be willing*, are quoted with one small difference. This time the word אולי appears in its full form, with a *vav*. One cannot help but wonder why Eliezer's implied self-interest wasn't expressed in this verse as well.

Analyzing Eliezer's innermost thoughts, we understand that at first he was totally unaware of having any personal interest in the matter. When performing an altruistic task, a

[כד:לט] ואמר אל אדני אלי לא תלך האשה אחרי.
[24:39] **And I said to my master: "Perhaps the woman will not wish to follow me."**

TORAH TREASURES • *Chayai-Sarah*

person is completely blind to any ulterior motives he may have. He is firmly convinced that his intentions are based on the highest ideals only. After Eliezer concluded that "the matter had proceeded from Hashem," that Rivkah would surely be married to Yitzchak, and that any hopes he had entertained regarding his own daughter were false, only then did he come to the realization, that at the very outset, when he had said to Avraham "אולי לא תאבה האשה," *"perhaps the woman will not be willing,"* he had had his personal interest at heart.

Rabbi Menachem Mendel of Kotzk

[כד:נב] ויהי כאשר שמע עבד אברהם את דבריהם וישתחו ארצה לה'.

[24:52] **And then, when the servant of Avraham heard their words, he prostrated himself on the ground before Hashem.**

... וישתחו ארצה לה'

... and he prostrated himself on the ground before Hashem

At first, when Eliezer spoke with Rivkah at the well, it says (24:26), "Then the man bowed his head and prostrated himself to Hashem."

Why is the word ארצה, *to the ground*, used in verse 52, yet missing in verse 26?

According to the *Gemara*, Eliezer was a learned man, a fact implied in his name דמשק אליעזר, דמשק being a contraction of the words דולה ומשקה, *he drew water and provided water*. That is to say, he taught others the teachings of his master. (*Yoma* 28)

This being so, he surely had learned from Avraham that the Torah forbids one to prostrate himself on a "figured stone" (*Vayikra* 26:1), even when worshipping Hashem.

Consequently, at the well, where the ground is not paved with stones, it says, "He prostrated himself before Hashem," whereas in Lavan's house, the Torah places the stress on ארצה, *to the ground*, and not on the stone floor. The reason for this is the Torah's

חיי שרה • TORAH TREASURES

prohibition against "figured stone."
Meshech Chochmah

ולבני הפילגשים אשר לאברהם נתן אברהם מתנת . . .
But to the children of the concubines of Avraham, Avraham gave gifts . . .

Rashi comments: The word הפילגשים, *the concubines*, appears in the abbreviated form, without a י, *yud*, (author's note: the standard text does contain a *yud*), because he had only one concubine, Hagar and Keturah being one and the same person.

The question arises: If indeed he had only one concubine, why the suffix ם, *mem*, which denotes the plural?

The solution to this problem may be found in the *Gemara (Sanhedrin* 21) which states: "Wives are those whom a man marries with a *kesubah*, a marriage contract, but concubines have no *kesubah*."

Furthermore, the *Gemara Sotah* 17 states: "The Divine Presence rests between husband (איש) and wife (אשה)." This latter *Gemara* can be explained as follows:

The word איש, *husband* contains the letter י, *yud*, while אשה, *wife* contains a ה, *hei*. Add to these the letters ו, *vav*, and ה, *hei*, which are included in the word כתובה. The resultant word is the שם הוי"ה, the Divine Name, the Tetragrammaton. That is the true meaning of "the Divine Presence rests between husband and wife."

By contrast, a concubine, being married without a כתובה, misses the *vav* and *hei*, half of the Divine Name. Etymologically, this may be reflected in the word פלגשם, as a contraction of פלג שם, *half a name*.

Vilna Gaon

[כה:ו] ולבני הפילגשים אשר לאברהם נתן אברהם מתנת וישלחם מעל יצחק בנו בעודנו חי קדמה אל ארץ קדם.

[25:6] But to the children of the concubines of Avraham, Avraham gave gifts, and while he still lived, he sent them away from his son Yitzchak eastward, to the land of the east.

63

Toldos / תולדות

... ותהר רבקה אשתו
... and Rivkah, his wife, conceived

It is surprising that the final segment of the verse reads, "And Rivkah, his wife, conceived," whereas the first part states, "Yitzchak entreated Hashem concerning his wife," without mentioning her name. Since the name Rivkah does not appear in the initial clause, we do not expect it in the final one either.

It is even more astounding, inasmuch as Rivkah was barren, that her name was not changed, especially in view of the fact that Sarah's conception at ninety years of age was attributable to the change of her name from Sarai to Sarah (17:15-16). We can readily understand that Yitzchak's name remained unchanged, because this name was assigned to him by Hashem, as it says, "And you shall call his name Yitzchak." But Rivkah's name could have been changed, yet it was not, which makes her conception all the more remarkable.

That is exactly the idea the Torah wishes to

[כה:כא] ויעתר יצחק לה' לנכח אשתו כי עקרה היא ויעתר לו ה' ותהר רבקה אשתו.

[25:21] **And Yitzchak entreated Hashem concerning his wife, for she was barren, and Hashem was entreated by him, and Rivka, his wife, conceived.**

convey by adding the name Rivkah to the phrase "and Rivkah, his wife, conceived." Even though her name was not changed, Yitzchak's prayers were accepted by Hashem, and Rivkah, with her original given name, conceived.

Chomas Anoch

[כה:כא] **ויעתר יצחק לה' לנכח אשתו כי עקרה היא ויעתר לו ה' ותהר רבקה אשתו.**

[25:21] **And Yitzchak entreated Hashem concerning his wife, for she was barren, and Hashem was entreated by him, and Rivka, his wife, conceived.**

ויעתר יצחק לה' לנכח אשתו כי עקרה היא ...
And Yitzchak entreated Hashem concerning his wife, for she was barren ...

The Hebrew phrase for "concerning his wife," לנכח אשתו, is somewhat obscure and gives rise to varied interpretations.

Rashbam renders it "for his wife," for her benefit. *Meshech Chochmah* elaborates that Yitzchak was assured he would have offspring. His certainty was based on Hashem's promise to Avraham: "You shall call his name Yitzchak, with him I will keep up my covenant for an everlasting covenant for his offspring after him." (17:19)

This promise did not preclude the possibility of another woman bearing his offspring. Thus, Yitzchak's prayer was לנכח אשתו, *for his wife*, specifically referring to Rivkah, meaning that Rivkah be the mother of his child, rather than someone else.

Otzar Chaim

ויעתר לו ה' ...
and Hashem was entreated by him ...

The implication in this verse is that Hashem answered only Yitzchak's prayer, not Rivkah's.

An explanation for this can be found in *Gemara Yevamos* 64: "The prayer of a *tzaddik* who is the son of a *tzaddik* is more effective than that of a *tzaddik* whose father is a wicked man."

The R'ash, in his responsa *Teshuvos Ha-r'ash*, answers a query, "When a community appoints a chazzan, should preference be given to a self-taught pious man or one of rabbinic ancestry?"

His response: "There is no benefit in a person's superior lineage; it is much better to befriend those who have been distant."

This decision, of course, contravenes the abovementioned *Gemara*.

Maharshal suggests the following reconciliation:

The prayer of a *tzaddik* who is himself the son of a *tzaddik* is more productive when he prays on his own behalf, for then the merit of his ancestors aids him. In praying for others, however, the opposite holds true, for then Hashem much prefers the prayers of those who turn away from the evil deeds of their fathers and, instead, walk in the path of righteousness.

Pardas Yosef

[כה:כב] ויתרצצו הבנים בקרבה ותאמר אם כן למה זה אנכי ותלך לדרש את ה'.

ויתרצצו הבנים בקרבה . . .
And the children struggled within her . . .

Rabbi Yissachar Dov of Belz poses the following question: It is quite understandable that Eisav struggled to leave his mother's womb, for inherently he was drawn to idolatry; yet, while in his mother's womb he was taught Torah by an angel, and this he simply could not endure. However, since Yaakov was also learning from an angel, why did he strive to come into the world?

Answers Rabbi Yissachar Dov: This teaches us that Yaakov was willing to forego learning Torah from an angel, if this entailed living in close proximity to Eisav.

Otzar Chaim

[25:22] And the children struggled within her, and she said: "If it be so, why do I live?" And she went to inquire of Hashem.

TORAH TREASURES • *Toldos*

[כה:כז] ויגדלו
הנערים ויהי עשו איש
ידע ציד איש שדה ויעקב
איש תם ישב אהלים.

[25:27] When the boys grew up, it came to pass that Eisav was a man who understood hunting, a man of the field, and Yaakov was a quiet man, living in tents.

ויהי עשו איש יודע ציד . . .
Eisav was a man who understood hunting . . .

On the subject of hunting, we find a most enlightening responsum in *Noda Biyehudah*, final edition, Vol 12, Responsum 10:

Question: There is a landowner who possesses large tracts of forest land teeming with wildlife. Is this landowner permitted to hunt and shoot wild game or is hunting per se forbidden, either because of the prohibition against *tzar baalei chaim*, the infliction of unnecessary pain on living creatures, or because of *baal tashchis*, the prohibition against wanton destruction?

Response: There is no *Halachic* prohibition against hunting wild life. Nevertheless, I have serious reservations concerning the ethical aspects of this activity. The only references in the Torah to hunting occur in context with Nimrod and Eisav.

(Author's note: Nimrod, the mighty Babylonian king, incited the entire world to rebellion against Hashem, as noted by Rashi in *Beraishis* 10:8, and concerning him it says (*ibid.* 10:9), "He was the mighty hunter before Hashem." The reference to Eisav's hunting is made in the above mentioned verse 25:27. Hence, hunting is associated with two distinctly un-Jewish personalities.)

It is not an activity befitting the children of Avraham, Yitzchak and Yaakov. All in all, hunting is inherently reprehensible, because it involves cruelty and exposes the hunter to physical danger. Therefore, my advice is that he remain at home, in safety, security and tranquility, and not waste his time on such things.

Iturei Torah

תולדות • TORAH TREASURES

ויגדלו הנערים . . .
When the boys grew up . . .

The *Midrash* tells us that for 13 years Yaakov and Eisav went to the same school and attended the same classes. Upon reaching the age of 13, one (Yaakov) turned to the *Beis Hamidrash*, while the other one (Eisav) made his way to the houses of idol-worship.

Rabbi Eliezer concludes from this that a father must care for his son until he reaches thirteen years of age. At his *Bar Mitzvah* he recites: *Baruch sheptarani mai'onsho shel zeh.* "Blessed be the One who has freed me from the punishment due this boy." This is because until his *Bar mitzvah* the father was responsible for his son's behavior and liable for his shortcomings.

The *Levush* adds another insight into this *berachah*. Until the *Bar Mitzvah*, the child could have suffered for the failures of the parents. This is in accordance with the *Gemara Kesuvos* 8, which expounds the verse in *Devarim* 32:19, "And Hashem saw and spurned, because of the provoking of his sons and daughters," meaning, when parents despise Hashem, He vents His anger on their children, and they die young.

Sifrei offers a similar explanation for the verse in *Devarim* 24:16, "Every man shall be put to death for his own sin," meaning, adults die for their sins, and children die for the sins of their parents.

This being the case, the *Bar Mitzvah* boy, rather than the father, should be the one to recite the *berachah*, for he is being released from the retribution he might suffer as a result of his parents' failures. Nevertheless, even according to the interpretation of the *Levush*, the father recites the *berachah*, for he

[כה:כז] ויגדלו
הנערים ויהי עשו איש
ידע ציד איש שדה ויעקב
איש תם ישב אהלים.

[25:27] When the boys grew up, it came to pass that Eisav was a man who understood hunting, a man of the field, and Yaakov was a quiet man, living in tents.

TORAH TREASURES • *Toldos*

[כה:ל] ויאמר עשו אל יעקב הלעיטני נא מן האדם האדם הזה כי עיף אנכי על כן קרא שמו אדום.
[25:30] And Eisav said to Yaakov: "Please let me drink my fill of this red stew, for I am faint." Therefore was his name called Edom.

[כו:טז] ויאמר אבימלך אל יצחק לך מעמנו כי עצמת ממנו מאד.
[26:16] And Avimelech said to Yitzchak: "Go away from us, for you have become much too strong for us."

is grateful that his own sins will no longer be visited upon his child.

Yalkut Yehudah

הלעיטני נא מן האדם הזה . . .
Please let me drink my fill of this red stew . . .

The first letters of the words הלעיטני נא מן, *please let me drink my fill of*, form an acrostic of the name המן, *Haman*, thereby alluding to a striking parallel. Just as Yaakov bought Eisav's birthright for bread and a pottage of lentils, so did Mordechai acquire Haman as his servant for a morsel of bread.

Baal Haturim

. . . לך מעמנו כי עצמת ממנו מאד
. . . go away from us, for you have become much too strong for us

In this verse the Torah reveals the true motive for anti-Semitism; it is rooted in the gentiles' perception that "you have become much too strong for us."

Chafetz Chaim

Author's note:
Taking the Chafetz Chaim's observation one step further, we realize that anti-Semitism is sparked not only by envy of Jewish wealth and possessions but also by jealousy of Jewish spiritual values. Chazal expressed this idea very succinctly when they stated: "Why was the mountain named Sinai? Because from this mountain *sin'ah*, hatred, descended upon the world." This means that the nations of the world were jealous of the Torah-qualities with which Israel was endowed.

התולדות • TORAH TREASURES

הקל קול יעקב והידים ידי עשו
The voice is the voice of Yaakov, and the hands, the hands of Eisav

The *Midrash* expounds: "Whenever the voice of Yaakov is heard, the hands of Eisav are powerless."

At first glance, the text would seem to indicate that the "voice of Yaakov" and "the hands of Eisav" will prevail simultaneously, contrary to the interpretation of the *Midrash*. However, upon closer examination, a deeper meaning emerges.

In the verse, קול, *voice*, appears in the abbreviated form, without a ו, *vav*. As such, it can also be read as קל, meaning unsteady or timid. Consequently, the verse can be interpreted as follows, in accordance with the *Midrash*: If the voice of Yaakov is קל, i.e. unsteadfast and halfhearted, then the hand of Eisav will prevail. On the other hand, if the voice of Yaakov is קול, in its *mallai* or full form, meaning resolute and vigorous, then the hands of Eisav are indeed powerless.

Vilna Gaon

... גם ברוך יהיה
... indeed, he shall remain blessed

Rashi, in his commentary on verse 27:36, explains: Why did Yitzchak tremble? He thought that perhaps he might have sinned in blessing the younger before the elder, thus changing the order of relationship between them. But then Eisav cried out, "For he has tricked me these two times." His father asked him, "What did he do to you?" Eisav replied, "He took away my birthright." Thereupon, Yitzchak said, "It was on account of this that I was troubled, because I thought I might have

[כז:כב] ויגש יעקב אל יצחק אביו וימשהו ויאמר הקל קול יעקב והידים ידי עשו.

[27:22] And Yaakov went near to Yitzchak his father, and he felt him and said: "The voice is the voice of Yaakov, and the hands, the hands of Eisav."

[כז:לג] ויחרד יצחק חרדה גדלה עד מאד ויאמר מי אפוא הוא הצד ציד ויבא לי ואכל מכל בטרם תבוא ואברכהו גם ברוך יהיה.

[27:33] And Yitzchak was seized by a very great tremor, and he said: "Who then is he that has hunted game and brought it to me, and I have eaten of all before you came, and I have blessed him? Indeed, he shall remain blessed!"

71

TORAH TREASURES • *Toldos*

overstepped the line of strict justice. Now, however, I realize that I blessed the firstborn, and he shall indeed remain blessed."

Accordingly, we can understand why the seemingly unnecessary word גם is used in the phrase גם ברוך יהיה. It denotes Yitzchak's affirmation of Yaakov's birthright. By adding the word גם he wished to imply: "I herewith acknowledge and confirm Yaakov's birthright."

Nachal Kedumim

[כז:מא] וישטם עשו את יעקב על הברכה אשר ברכו אביו ויאמר עשו בלבו יקרבו ימי אבל אבי ואהרגה את יעקב אחי.

[27:41] **And Eisav hated Yaakov because of the blessing with which his father blessed him, and Eisav said in his heart: "The days of mourning for my father are near, then I will slay my brother Yaakov."**

וישטם עשו את יעקב על הברכה אשר ברכו אביו . . .
And Eisav hated Yaakov because of the blessing with which his father blessed him . . .

Rabbi Yonassan Eibeschutz frames his commentary on this verse in the form of a question. Why is it, he wonders, that when a rabbi declares an animal to be *treifah*, the butcher does not raise his voice in protest or otherwise show contempt for the rabbi; he simply abides by the rabbi's decision and absorbs his loss. By contrast, if the same butcher was involved in a dispute over a business matter and the rabbi finds that he owes money, even if it concerns only a paltry sum, he will object strenuously, accuse the rabbi of being unfair and do all he can to avoid complying with the rabbi's ruling.

He answers with keen insight into human nature. When the rabbi declares an animal *treifa*, the butcher indeed suffers the loss, but no one gains from the butcher's misfortune. However, if the rabbi finds the butcher liable to pay even a small amount, someone else will receive his money. This fact is the source of the butcher's unhappiness.

The same holds true for Eisav. He hated Yaakov, not for the fact that he, Eisav, *did not* receive the blessing; he hated him "because of the blessing with which his father blessed him," because Yaakov *did* receive the blessing.

Otzar Chaim

ויקרא יצחק אל יעקב ויברך אתו ויצוהו ויאמר לו לא תקח אשה מבנות כנען
And Yitzchak called Yaakov and blessed him, and commanded him and said to him: "Do not take a wife from the daughters of Canaan"

With this passage, the Torah teaches us a lesson in pedagogy.

The way to guide a child in the desired direction is not by intimidation, threats and displays of anger. The proper approach is by emulating Yitzchak's method, as it manifests itself in this verse.

Initially, he "blessed him," that is to say, he spoke gently to him, thereby creating a cordial atmosphere. Only after the blessing did he ask him not to "take a wife from the daughters of Canaan."

Chafetz Chaim

[כח:א] ויקרא יצחק אל יעקב ויברך אתו ויצוהו ויאמר לו לא תקח אשה מבנות כנען.

[28:1] **And Yitzchak called Yaakov and blessed him, and commanded him and said to him: "Do not take a wife from the daughters of Canaan."**

Vayaitzai / ויצא

ויצא יעקב ...
And Yaakov went out ...

The word ויצא, *and he went out*, implies that he left behind a void. As Rashi explains, a *tzaddik's* departure leaves an imprint. The question, therefore, arises: Avraham also left his father's house. Yet, in recounting Avraham's departure (12:4) the Torah uses the word וילך, *and he went*. Why not ויצא, as with Yaakov?

The answer is that when Yaakov left the home of Yitzchak and Rivkah, his departure and absence were keenly felt, because they valued his greatness and his splendid character. On the other hand, when Avraham departed, he left an environment of idolators who did not appreciate his outstanding qualities. As a result, when he left they did not sense that "the splendor and radiance of their town had departed with him," and the word ויצא would thus not be appropriate.

Chasam Sofer

[כח:י] ויצא יעקב מבאר שבע וילך חרנה.

[28:10] And Yaakov went out from Be'er Sheva and went towards Charan.

TORAH TREASURES • *Vayaitzai*

[כח:י] ויצא יעקב מבאר שבע וילך חרנה.

[28:10] And Yaakov went out from Be'er Sheva and went towards Charan.

ויצא יעקב מבאר שבע וילך חרנה
And Yaakov went out from Be'er Sheva and went towards Charan

Why does the Torah tell us that Yaakov went out of Be'er Sheva, something seemingly irrelevant, since we are primarily interested in his destination?

The Dubna Maggid suggests the following reason: A person undertakes a journey either because he is forced to leave his present locality or because he wishes to go to a different locality. In the case of Yaakov's journey to Charan both of these reasons applied. Rivkah told Yaakov to leave Be'er Sheva because Eisav wanted to kill him. Yitzchak, however, told him to go to Charan for an entirely different reason. He said, "Arise, go to Paddan Aram... and take a wife from the daughters of Lavan." He was to go there to find a wife.

Thus we find that both his departure from home and his destination were important elements of his journey. It is for this reason that the Torah stresses both ויצא, *he went out*, and וילך, *he went to*.

Otzar Chaim

[כח:כב] והאבן הזאת אשר שמתי מצבה יהיה בית אלקים וכל אשר תתן לי עשר אעשרנו לך.

[28:22] And this stone which I have set as a memorial shall become a house of the Lord, and everything You will give me, I shall repeatedly tithe to You.

... עשר אעשרנו לך
... I shall repeatedly tithe to you

Alshich interprets the double use of the word עשר in this verse as referring to a double *maaser*, tenth, i.e. a *chomash*, a fifth.

This *chomash* is the subject of a rabbinic dictum which states: המבזבז אל יבזבז יותר מחומש. Anyone who lavishly spends his money (for *tzedakah*) should not spend more than one fifth of his wealth.

An allusion to this statement may be found in the numerical equivalence of עשר אעשרנו

ויצא • TORAH TREASURES

וזה כל המבזבז אל יבזבז יותר מחומש and
Memayanos Hanetzach

ויאמר הן עוד היום גדול . . .
And he said: "Behold, it is still the middle of the day . . ."

Yaakov's words give us reason to wonder. What was he trying to tell the shepherds? Did they themselves not know that it was the middle of the day?

Yaakov's statement can be understood if we remember that on the previous day Hashem had caused the sun to set early in order to induce Yaakov to spend the night at the site of the future *Bais Hamikdash*.

This unusually early sunset forced the shepherds to gather their sheep in darkness. In order to avoid this from occurring again, this day they rounded up their flocks much earlier. Therefore, when Yaakov noticed what they were planning to do, he assured them that there were still many daylight hours left. This day, the sun would not set early again. Consequently, "it is not yet time that the sheep should be gathered together."

Avnei Shoham

[כט:ז] ויאמר הן עוד היום גדול לא עת האסף המקנה השקו הצאן ולכו רעו.

[29:7] And he said: "Behold, it is still the middle of the day. It is not yet time that the sheep should be gathered together. Give the sheep to drink and take them to pasture."

. . . ויספר ללבן את כל הדברים האלה
. . . and he told Lavan all these things

Rashi, on verse 29:11, tells us that Elifaz, the son of Eisav, acting on his father's command, pursued Yaakov in order to kill him. However, Elifaz had been brought up by Yitzchak and could not bring himself to commit murder. He said to Yaakov, "But what shall I do regarding my father's command?" Yaakov replied: "Take all my possessions making me a poor man, and

[כט:יג] ויהי כשמע לבן את שמע יעקב בן אחתו וירץ לקראתו ויחבק לו וינשק לו ויביאהו אל ביתו ויספר ללבן את כל הדברים האלה.

[29:13] And when Lavan heard the tidings of Yaakov, his sister's son, he ran to

77

TORAH TREASURES • *Vayaitzai*

meet him, and he embraced him and kissed him, and brought him to his house and he told Lavan all these things.

a poor man is not considered living."

The words את כל הדברים האלה, *all these things*, form the acronym of the initial letters of the words in the sentence expressing what Yaakov told Lavan: אל תתפלא כי לא הבאתי דבר ברכוש רב יצאתי מביתי הלך אליפז לקח הכל. *Do not be surprised that I came empty-handed. I left my home with great wealth, but Elifaz came and took it all away.*

Vilna Gaon

[כט:לד] ותהר עוד ותלד בן ותאמר עתה הפעם ילוה אישי אלי כי ילדתי לו שלשה בנים על כן קרא שמו לוי.

[29:34] And she conceived again and bore a son, and she said: "This time will my husband be joined to me, because I have borne him three sons." Therefore, he was called Levi.

... עתה הפעם ילוה אישי אלי כי ילדתי לו שלשה בנים
"This time will my husband be joined to me, because I have borne him three sons..."

Until now I was in the habit of leading my two small sons with my two hands, but now that I have given birth to a third son, my husband will have to help me lead them.

Chizkuni

[ל:יח] ותאמר לאה נתן אלקים שכרי אשר נתתי שפחתי לאישי ותקרא שמו יששכר.

[30:18] And Leah said: "The Lord has given me my reward because I gave my handmaiden to my husband." And she named him Yissachar.

... ותקרא שמו יששכר
... and she named him Yissachar

According to the Massoretic text transmitted to us from generation to generation, throughout the Torah the name יששכר is spelled with a double ש, *sin*. The first one is punctuated with a *dagesh* and a *kametz*, but the second is silent, belonging to the category of letters "which are written, but not pronounced."

The Chasam Sofer advances a thought-provoking reason for the appearance of this silent *sin*. He uses as a premise the explanation by the Rashba who offers a reason for the name Yissachar being spelled with two *sins*. Leah saw in his birth a reward for two actions. (The root of Yissachar is the word *sachar*, reward.) One was the reward for "giving her handmaid to her husband." (*Beraishis* 30:18) The second reward was for the *duda'im*, the wildflowers Leah gave Rachel in exchange for her husband that night. (*ibid.* 30:16) In both these verses the word *sachar* appears.

The Chasam Sofer explains that it would have been unseemly for Leah to mention the second reward, for it carried the disparaging implication that Rachel surrendered her rights to her husband for a bunch of flowers. Merely hinting at the *duda'im* would make Leah guilty of "deriving glory from another person's downfall," and as such "she would have no share in the World to Come." Therefore, Leah kept the *duda'im* reason to herself, announcing only the second reward. Hence, the second *sin* in Yissachar remains silent.

Otzar Chaim

... ותקרא שמו יששכר
... and she named him Yissachar

Rashi tells us (*Beraishis* 29:25) that Yaakov, suspecting that Lavan might substitute Leah for Rachel, gave Rachel certain secret identifying signs. Rachel, however, could not bear to let her sister Leah suffer embarrassment. Therefore, with supreme self-sacrifice, she informed Leah of the signs. Thus, Rachel became the symbol of sublime self-denial.

Mahara of Worms points out that the numerical value of יששכר, *Yissachar*, equals that of the words רחל מסרה ללאה סימנין, *Rachel handed over the identifying signs to Leah*. What is the connection between this allusion and the name Yissachar?

The explanation is as follows: In naming her son Yissachar, Leah noted her awareness that

[ל:יח] ותאמר לאה נתן אלקים שכרי אשר נתתי שפחתי לאישי ותקרא שמו יששכר.

[30:18] And Leah said: "The Lord has given me my reward because I gave my handmaiden to my husband." And she named him Yissachar.

his birth represented a reward, either for the *duda'im*, the wildflowers, she gave to Rachel or for giving her handmaiden Zilpah to Yaakov (cf. previous commentary). The aforementioned *gematria* hints at the fact that his birth was attributable chiefly to Rachel's magnanimity, without which Leah would never have become Yaakov's wife. Until Yissachar, Leah had not ascribed the birth of any of her children to her own deeds. However, since she did attribute the birth of Yissachar to her own merits, the Torah, by means of this *gematria*, set the record straight.

A similar *gematria* corroborates the supreme nobility of Rachel's character:

The *Navi* tells us that at the time of the destruction of the *Bais Hamikdash*, Rachel pleaded with Hashem for the Jewish people, in the merit of having overcome her own innate tendencies by not being envious of her sister Leah. And Hashem replied: . . . מנעי קולך מבכי כי יש שכר לפעולתך. *Hold back your voice from weeping . . . for your work shall be rewarded.* (*Yirmiyah* 31:16)

The numerical value of יש שכר, *shall be rewarded*, equals that of רחל מסרה ללאה סימנין, *Rachel handed over the identifying signs to Leah*. This *gematria* indicates Hashem's concurrence with Rachel's claim and His pledge that her work "would be rewarded".

Nachal Kedumim

[ל:כז] ויאמר אליו לבן אם נא מצאתי חן בעיניך נחשתי ויברכני ה' בגללך.

[30:27] **And Lavan said to him: "If only I have found favor in your eyes, I have made a divination and learned that Hashem has blessed me for your sake."**

. . . ויברכני ה' בגללך
. . . that Hashem has blessed me for your sake

This phrase may be interpreted as follows: "From the moment that you rolled away the stone from the opening of the well, Hashem's blessing was bestowed on all my undertakings."

Rabbeinu Ephraim

Author's Note: The Hebrew term used here is בגללך, *for your sake*. The root of this word is גלל, *to roll*. Thus, the etymological development is בגללך: you started it rolling, you caused it, for your sake. According to Rabbeinu Ephraim's rendering, Lavan alludes to the literal meaning of בגללך, *through your rolling*, meaning, "from the moment you rolled away the stone."

וישלח יעקב ויקרא לרחל וללאה השדה אל צאנו
And Yaakov sent and called Rachel and Leah to the field, to his flock

A husband, though he is the head of the household, should not impose his authority nor use intimidation on his wife and family. Rather, he should use persuasion and gentle reasoning to induce them to follow his suggestions.

This mild and amiable approach was employed by Yaakov when speaking to his wives. He had the clearly expressed mandate of Hashem "to return to the land of your fathers." (31:3) Yet, broaching the subject of returning, he slowly introduced the idea to Rachel and Leah, reviewing the entire history of his stay with Lavan, devoting ten verses to the process. (31:4-14) All this, in order to make them amenable to his proposed plan.

Sheloh Hakadosh

עתה קום צא ...
Now arise, go out ...

Initially, Yaakov rationalized his wish to

TORAH TREASURES • *Vayaitzai*

הארץ הזאת ושוב אל
ארץ מולדתך.

[31:13] **I am the Lord of Beis El where you anointed a memorial and where you made a vow to Me; now arise, go out of this land to the land of your birth."**

escape from Lavan by explaining to Rachel and Leah that Lavan had "changed my wages ten times," a clear indictment of Lavan's unfairness and greed. Only at the conclusion did he mention Hashem's command that he leave.

Yaakov did this in order to diminish the aspect of "divine test," so as not to expose himself to a trial by Hashem.

Similarly, Rachel and Leah, when consenting to leave, express their agreement in commonplace terms that diminish the aspect of "divine test." Their first response is: "Have we still any portion or inheritance in the house of our father? Are we not considered by him as strangers, for he sold us?" Meaning, common sense dictates that we leave. Having said that, they conclude, "So do now whatever Hashem had told you to do."

The lesson to be learned is that we must lessen our exposure to a "divine test" as much as possible.

Rabbi Simchah Zissel of Kelm

Vayishlach / וישלח

... עם לבן גרתי ואחר עד עתה
... I have stayed with Lavan and have tarried until now

Rabbi Chaim of Sanz, the illustrious Chassidic Rebbe, was seated at his saintly table. Engrossed in deep thought, he seized his long white beard and sighed: "עם לבן גרתי, *my beard has turned white* (a play on the word לבן, which also means white); ואחר עד עתה, *and I have tarried so long and still not repented.*"

Memayenos Hanetzach

ויאמר אם יבוא עשו אל המחנה האחת והכהו ...
And he said: "If Eisav comes to one camp and destroys it ..."

The word והכהו, *and destroys it*, in the Hebrew is a palindrome, i.e. a word reading the same backward as forward, signifying that whoever inflicts harm on Yisrael will ultimately suffer harm himself.

Da'as Chachamim

[לב:ה] ויצו אתם לאמר כה תאמרון לאדני לעשו כה אמר עבדך יעקב עם לבן גרתי ואחר עד עתה.

[32:5] And he commanded them saying: "Thus shall you say to my lord Eisav. Thus says your servant Yaakov, As a stranger have I stayed with Lavan and have tarried until now."

[לב:ט] ויאמר אם יבוא עשו אל המחנה האחת והכהו והיה המחנה הנשאר לפליטה.

[32:9] And he said: "If Eisav comes to one camp and destroys it then the camp that is left shall escape."

TORAH TREASURES • *Vayishlach*

ויאמר אם יבוא עשו אל המחנה האחת והכהו...
And he said: "If Eisav comes to one camp and destroys it..."

Rashi explains that by dividing his entourage into two camps, Yaakov was guaranteed that, in the event of a battle, there would be survivors. The question arises: While Yaakov's action may have increased the chances for survival, in what way did they constitute a guarantee? Wasn't it possible that, Heaven forbid, both camps would be annihilated?

According to the *Midrash*, the two camps were one day's journey apart. Yaakov himself stayed with the forward camp, ready to face Eisav on the battlefield.

Yaakov knew that he and Eisav were destined to die on the same day, as had indeed been prophecied by Rivkah when she said, "Why should I lose both of you on the same day?" (*Beraishis* 27:45) Therefore, if Eisav succeeded in destroying the forward camp, thereby killing Yaakov, Eisav himself would also die that day, and the second camp which was a day's journey distant, would be spared. This was Yaakov's guarantee.

Chanukas Hatorah

[לב:יא] קטנתי מכל החסדים ומכל האמת אשר עשית את עבדך כי במקלי עברתי את הירדן הזה ועתה הייתי לשני מחנות.

[32:11] "I am unworthy of all the kindness and of all the truth which You have shown to Your servant, for with my staff I passed over this Jordan, and now I have become two camps."

קטנתי מכל החסדים ומכל האמת...
I am unworthy of all the kindness and of all the truth...

This verse is the eighth verse in *Parshas Vayishlach*, which in turn is the eighth *parshah* in *Beraishis*.

This may allude to the Talmudic aphorism (*Sotah* 5a) which states that a scholar should have one eighth of an eighth measure of haughtiness. This much, but not more.

Beyond the one eighth of an eighth, he must

say, "קטנתי, *I am unworthy."*

Vilna Gaon

הצלני נא מיד אחי מיד עשו ...
Deliver me, I pray, from the hand of my brother, from the hand of Eisav ...

Yaakov feared not only "the hand of Eisav" but, equally, "the hand of my brother," of his holding out the right hand of friendship, of his excessive cordiality.

The "hand of Eisav" imperils Yaakov physically, but even more alarming than that is "the hand of my brother," his brotherhood, his fellowship, which expose the spirit and soul of Yaakov to mortal danger.

Bais Halevi

[לב:יב] הצילני נא מיד אחי מיד עשו כי ירא אנכי אתו פן יבוא והכני אם על בנים.

[32:12] "Deliver me, I pray, from the hand of my brother, from the hand of Eisav, for I fear him, lest he come and destroy us, mother and children alike."

ויעקב נסע סכתה ...
And Yaakov journeyed to Sukkos ...

According to the *Halachah* (*Zevachim* 16b) a maimed person is prohibited from offering a sacrifice.

Yaakov, being maimed, since "he limped from his thigh," was not permitted to erect an altar when he journeyed to Sukkos. He merely "built a house for himself and made booths for his cattle."

On the other hand, when he arrived שלם, *in undiminished completeness*, at the city of Shechem, which Rashi expounds as meaning "whole in his body, for he was healed from his limping," he immediately built an altar and offered a sacrifice.

Meshech Chochmah

Author's note:

It seems that *Meshech Chochmah's* commentary is in conflict with the *Midrash* quoted

[לג:יז] ויעקב נסע סכתה ויבן לו בית ולמקנהו עשה סכת על כן קרא שם המקום סכות.

[33:17] And Yaakov journeyed to Sukkos and built a house for himself and made booths for his cattle. Therefore, the name of the place is called Sukkos.

by Rashi (*ibid.* 32:32) "that the sun shone for his benefit to heal his limping when he had passed Penuel." The verse continues, "And he limped from his thigh." This refers to the time when the sun began to shine, but a moment after that, the sun had accomplished the healing process (see *Sifsei Chachamim*). It follows that at Penuel, Yaakov was already healed and when he came to Sukkos he could have offered a sacrifice.

‏. . . ויבאו על העיר בטח
. . . they came upon the city unawares

The word ‏בטח, *unawares*, in the context of this verse can also be translated as confident, referring to Shimon and Levi's confident frame of mind. What was the source of their confidence? What emboldened these two men to launch an assault on an entire city?

Yaakov's sons knew that the people of Shechem, in case of war, could count on the entire world to come to their aid. They were equally convinced that no one would lift a finger to rescue Shechem after their circumcision. This certainly inspired their confidence to march on the city, knowing full well that circumcision would make the men of Shechem outcasts in the eyes of the world.

Kli Yakar

‏[לד:כה] ויהי ביום השלישי בהיותם כאבים ויקחו שני בני יעקב שמעון ולוי אחי דינה איש חרבו ויבאו על העיר בטח ויהרגו כל זכר.

[34:25] **And it came to pass on the third day, when they were in pain, that the two sons of Yaakov, Shimon and Levi, Dinah's brothers, took their swords and came upon the city unawares, and they killed all the males.**

‏ויאמר אלקים אל יעקב קום עלה בית־אל ושב שם ועשה שם מזבח . . .
And the Lord said to Yaakov: "Arise, go up to Bais El, and dwell there, and make there an altar . . ."

This verse is unusual in that it is the only place in the entire Torah where an individual is commanded to build an altar.

‏[לה:א] ויאמר אלקים אל יעקב קום עלה אל בית אל ושב שם ועשה שם מזבח לקל הנראה אליך בברחך מפני עשו אחיך.

[35:1] **And the Lord said to Yaakov: "Arise, go up to Bais**

ויוולח • TORAH TREASURES

A possible explanation for this singular command is suggested by *Meshech Chochmah*: Speaking on behalf of Hashem, Yeshayah Hanavi states: "For I, Hashem... hate robbery with iniquity." (*Yeshayah* 61:8) Yaakov was fearful of having acquired stolen goods from the spoils of Shechem, thus being disqualified from offering sacrifices to Hashem. However, Hashem laid these trepidations to rest, assuring him that his sacrifices would be accepted and that he is indeed permitted to erect an altar.

Meshech Chochmah

El, and dwell there, and make there an altar to the Lord who appeared to you when you fled before your brother Eisav."

... ישראל
... **Yisrael**

The Tashbatz (Rabbi Shimshon ben Tzadok), a disciple of the Maharam (Rabbi Meir of Rothenberg), writes that the name ישראל, *Yisrael*, forms an acrostic of the initials of all the names of the *Avos* and *Imahos*. The *yud* stands for Yitzchak and Yaakov, the *sin* for Sarah, the *reish* for Rivkah and Rachel, the *aleph* for Avraham and the *lamed* for Leah. The entire name Yisrael represents Klal Yisrael.

Chomas Anoch

[לה:י] ויאמר לו אלקים שמך יעקב לא יקרא שמך עוד יעקב כי אם ישראל יהיה שמך ויקרא את שמו ישראל.

[35:10] And the Lord said to him: "Your name is Yaakov, but your name shall no longer be Yaakov, but Yisrael shall be your name." And He called his name Yisrael.

... בשמת
Basemas ...

It is noteworthy that at the time Eisav married Basemas, the Torah calls her Machalas (28:9). Underlying this name change is the following thought:

When Eisav took Machalas as a wife all his sins were forgiven, according to the statement of our Sages that a person is forgiven all his

[לו:ג] ואת בשמת בת ישמעאל אחות נביות.

[36:3] And Basemas, Yishmael's daughter, sister of Nevayos.

TORAH TREASURES • *Vayishlach*

[לו:ג] ואת בשמת בת ישמעאל אחות נביות.

[36:3] **And Basemas, Yishmael's daughter, sister of Nevayos.**

sins on his wedding day. Hence the name Machalas, a derivative of the verb *mochel*, which means to forgive. But Eisav persisted in his old ways of wickedness and rebellion against Hashem. Therefore, now the text calls her Basemas. The Hebrew name בשמת, divided into its syllables and read in reverse, yields the words שב מת. Based on the dictum that a wicked man is considered dead, these words indicate that Eisav persisted in his wicked ways.

Chomas Anoch

Vayaishev / וישב

המלך תמלך עלינו אם משול תמשל בנו
"Shall you indeed reign over us? Shall you indeed dominate us?"

The brothers use two phrases in this verse, *maloch timloch*, reign over, and *mashol timshol*, have dominion over. There is a well-known *Gemara* in *Berachos* 55b that tells us that dreams are fulfilled according to the interpretations of the interpreter. Therefore, in the case of Yosef, since the brothers interpreted his dreams as foreshadowing both *meluchah*, kingship, and *memshalah*, dominion, both of these came true.

Meluchah denotes monarchy, with the consent and approval of the governed, whereas *memshalah*, dominion, implies absolute rule of domination and dictatorship. Both aspects were actualized.

When the brothers came to Egypt and prostrated themselves before Yosef, they felt compelled to do so, thereby fulfilling Yosef's *memshalah* aspect of the dream. However, after the death of Yaakov, the brothers came to

[לז:ח] ויאמרו לו אחיו המלך תמלך עלינו אם משול תמשל בנו ויוספו עוד שנא אתו על חלמתיו ועל דבריו.

[37:8] **And his brothers said to him:** "Shall you indeed reign over us? Shall you indeed dominate us?" And they hated him yet the more for his dreams and for his words.

Yosef and said, "Behold, we are your servants." (*Beraishis* 50:18) This time they willingly accepted him as their king, in fulfillment of the *meluchah* aspect of his dream.

Rabbi Yitzchak Zev Soloveitchik

[לז:כב] ויאמר אלהם ראובן אל תשפכו דם השליכו אתו אל הבור הזה אשר במדבר ויד אל תשלחו בו למען הציל אתו מידם להשיבו אל אביו.

[37:22] **And Reuven said to them: "Shed no blood, cast him into this pit in the desert, but lay no hand on him," that he might deliver him from them and return him to his father.**

ויאמר אלהם ראובן אל תשפכו דם השליכו אתו אל הבור ...
And Reuven said to them: "Shed no blood, cast him into this pit ..."

This verse demands an explanation. How did Reuven expect to save Yosef? After all, the pit contained snakes and scorpions. The Vilna Gaon offers an ingenious answer.

The *Gemara* in *Shabbos* 21b brings two consecutive statements in the name of Rav Tanchum. The first is that a *Chanukah* lamp placed higher than twenty cubits is unfit for use. The second addresses the apparent redundancy in the verse, "And they took him and cast him into the pit, and the pit was empty, with no water in it." (37:24) Rav Tanchum explains that although there was no water in it, there were snakes and scorpions. The question presents itself: What is the connection between these consecutive but apparently unrelated statements?

At first glance, it seems difficult to understand that Reuven would tell his brothers to cast him into a pit filled with snakes and scorpions. The *Gemara* in *Yevamos* teaches that a woman whose husband was thrown into a pit containing snakes and scorpions is permitted to remarry since her husband could not possibly have survived. If so, how could Reuven suggest that they cast Yosef into a pit in which he would surely die? Yet, the Torah testifies that Reuven hoped "to deliver him from them." For an answer we must return to the

Gemara Shabbos 21b, which gives us the reason for the requirement that the *Chanukah* lamp be placed no higher than twenty cubits. The reason is that the human eye does not easily notice something twenty cubits away from eye level. There is also another *Gemara* in *Tamid* which states that the term "to throw" or "to cast" is applicable only if the distance over which the object is thrown exceeds twenty cubits.

Since Reuven suggested that they "cast" him into the pit, it follows that the pit was deeper than twenty cubits. And since the human eye does not observe any object that is beyond twenty cubits from eye level, it is only logical to assume that Reuven did not know that the pit contained snakes and scorpions.

The connection between Rav Tanchum's two statements suddenly becomes very clear. Only after we have established that twenty cubits beyond eye level is out of the normal field of vision can we understand how Reuven could suggest they cast Yosef into a pit which contained snakes and scorpions. He obviously had not seen them.

Vilna Gaon

ויאמר אלהם ראובן אל תשפכו דם השליכו אתו אל הבור ...
And Reuven said to them: "Shed no blood, cast him into this pit . . ."

The question arises: What did Reuven hope to gain by having Yosef cast into a pit full of snakes and scorpions?

The *Gemara* in *Berachos* 33 relates that in a certain place there was a venomous lizard which continually would bite man and beast. The people informed Rabbi Chanina ben Dosa of its existence. Rabbi Chanina placed his heel

[לז:כב] ויאמר אלהם ראובן אל תשפכו דם השליכו אתו אל הבור הזה אשר במדבר ויד אל תשלחו בו למען הציל אתו מידם להשיבו אל אביו.

[37:22] **And Reuven said to them: "Shed no blood, cast him into this pit in the desert, but lay no hand on him,"** that

TORAH TREASURES • *Vayaishev*

he might deliver him from them and return him to his father.

on the opening of the hole. The lizard came out, bit him and died instantly.

Rabbi Chanina ben Dosa explained: "You see, my children, it is not the serpent that kills, but the sins."

It was this very notion that inspired Reuven with the faith that the snakes and scorpions in the pit would not harm the righteous Yosef. And indeed, events proved him right, for Yosef emerged unscathed.

Rabbi Yitzchak Zev Soloveitchik

[לז:כד] ויקחהו וישלכו אתו הברה והבור רק אין בו מים.

[37:24] **And they took him and cast him into the pit, and the pit was empty, with no water in it.**

ויקחהו וישלכו אתו הברה והבור רק אין בו מים
And they took him and cast him into the pit, and the pit was empty, with no water in it

The word בור occurs two times in this verse, הברה, *into the pit,* and והבור, *and the pit*. The first appears in the abbreviated form, without a ו, *vav,* while the latter is spelled fully, with the *vav*.

The Vilna Gaon perceives this variance as an allusion in support of the statement in *Gemara Shabbos* 22 that the pit contained no water, but it did contain snakes and scorpions.

Now, according to the Ramban's commentary, Yosef's brothers knew the pit was empty of water, but they did not know that it contained snakes and scorpions. Therefore, when the Torah relates that they threw him into the pit, the abbreviated spelling is used to indicate their perception that the pit was totally empty. However, when the Torah narrates the true state of affairs it uses the full spelling to indicate that it did contain snakes and scorpions, and that the brothers should have examined the pit in order to ascertain if it was indeed as empty as they had presumed it to be.

Vilna Gaon

וישב • TORAH TREASURES

וימכרו את יוסף לישמעאלים בעשרים כסף...
And they sold Yosef to the Ishmaelites for twenty pieces of silver...

Targum Yonassan ben Uziel adds that they used the twenty pieces of silver to buy shoes. Likewise, in the moving prayer *Aileh Ezkarah* which is recited during *Mussaf* on *Yom Kippur*, the Roman emperor is quoted as saying to the ten martyrs: "What can you say in defense of your forefathers who sold their brother for a pair of shoes?" The source for both these references is *Amos* 2:6, "Because they sell the righteous for silver, and the needy for a pair of shoes." The connection, however, between the two seemingly unrelated elements—the selling of Yosef into slavery and the purchase of shoes—remains to be explained.

Upon reflection, the selling of Yosef into slavery was tantamount to a death sentence, both in the physical sense (a delicate young boy could not possibly survive the rigors of servitude) and the spiritual sense (being thrust from Yaakov's home into a pagan world would defile his pure soul). It would seem, therefore, that immediately subsequent to this incident a period of mourning over Yosef would be justified, were it not for the ruling in *Gemara Sanhedrin* which states that no mourning is observed for those sentenced and executed by law.

Yosef's brothers, viewing their action as fully in accordance with Torah law, and his certain death as death by execution, refused to mourn his passing. Since a mourner is forbidden to wear shoes, they demonstratively bought and wore shoes for all to see, thereby indicating that in the case of Yosef's "death", the laws of mourning do not apply.

Oznaim Latorah

[לז:כח] ויעברו אנשים מדינים סחרים וימשכו ויעלו את יוסף מן הבור וימכרו את יוסף לישמעאלים בעשרים כסף ויביאו את יוסף מצרימה.

[37:28] And Midianite men passed by, merchants, and they drew Yosef up out of the pit, and they sold Yosef to the Ishmaelites for twenty pieces of silver, and they brought Yosef to Egypt.

TORAH TREASURES • *Vayaishev*

[לז:כט-ל] וישב ראובן אל הבור והנה אין יוסף בבור ויקרע את בגדיו וישב אל אחיו ויאמר הילד איננו ואני אנה אני בא.

[37:29-30] And Reuven returned to the pit, and behold, Yosef was not in the pit, and he tore his garments asunder. And he returned to his brothers and said: "The boy is not there. And as for me, where can I go?"

וישב ראובן אל הבור . . .
And Reuven returned to the pit . . .

These verses can be interpreted homiletically as follows: *And Reuven returned to the pit . . .* When the hour approaches for a person to returns to the grave, and he sees that *behold, Yosef is not in the pit*, there are no additions in the grave (the word *Yosef* also means to add), no more Torah and *mitzvos*, he comes to the realization that *the boy is not there*, the days of youth, those wonderful days of building and achieving are gone forever. *And as for me, where can I go?* How will I merit entering the World to Come?

Al HaTorah

[לח:כג] ויאמר יהודה תקח לה פן נהיה לבוז הנה שלחתי הגדי הזה ואתה לא מצאתה.

[38:2] And Yehuda said: "Let her take it to herself, lest we be put to shame. See, I have sent this kid, and you have not found her."

פן נהיה לבוז . . .
lest we be put to shame . . .

Yehudah, speaking to his friend Chirah, uses the pronoun "we," even though Chirah, acting only as Yehudah's messenger, had not done anything shameful to have earned disgrace. This is a manifestation of the fact that a person's actions reflect on his friends, for better or worse. As the saying goes, "A person is known by the company he keeps."

Iturei Torah

[מ:ב] ויקצף פרעה על שני סריסיו על שר המשקים ועל שר האופים.

[40:2] And Pharaoh was angry with his two officers, with the chief of the butlers and with the chief of the bakers.

ויקצף פרעה על שני סריסיו . . .
And Pharaoh was angry with his two officers . . .

The *Gemara* in *Megillah* 13b comments that Hashem caused the master to grow angry with his servants in order to do the will of the righteous one, namely Yosef. It was through Hashem's intervention that both the butler and the baker offended Pharoah, which ultimately brought about Yosef's elevation to the high office of viceroy.

The question arises: Since only the butler was directly instrumental in Yosef's release from prison, why was it also necessary for the baker to commit an offense?

Let us reflect upon the butler's reasoning. Without the interpretation of the baker's dream, the butler would have doubted the interpretation of his own dream and, concomitantly, Yosef's ability to interpret dreams. Indeed, upon hearing only the good portents of his own dream, the butler would have concluded that Yosef had nothing to lose with this interpretation. If it came true, all was well. If it did not, who would hold him responsible?

However, the fact that Yosef foretold the baker's eventual execution convinced the butler of the divinely inspired character of the interpretations. It stood to reason that if Yosef's interpretations were spurious, he would not have dared predict the baker's death on the gallows. For if events proved him wrong, he would have to suffer the baker's terrible vengeance for having caused him so much anxiety. It followed, therefore, that Yosef spoke the truth. The butler's certainty that Yosef's interpretations were genuine prompted him to recommend Yosef to Pharoah, which led to his release and elevation.

Meshech Chochmah

וכוס פרעה בידי ...
And Pharaoh's cup was in my hand ...

[מ:יא] וכוס פרעה בידי ואקח את הענבים ואשחט אתם אל כוס פרעה ואתן את הכוס על כף פרעה.

[40:11] "And Pharaoh's cup was in my hand, and I took the

One of the reasons for drinking four cups of wine at the *Pesach Seder* is the four times the word *kos*, cup, occurs in the above verses.

The events surrounding the butler's dream and Yosef's interpretation of it were the seeds

grapes and pressed them into Pharaoh's cup, and I gave the cup into Pharaoh's hand."

from which sprouted the eventual redemption from Egyptian bondage, which we commemorate at the *Seder*.

Meiri

Mikaytz / מקץ

ויהי מקץ שנתים ימים ופרעה חלם...
And it came to pass, at the end of two full years that Pharaoh dreamed...

The *Midrash* on this verse quotes from *Iyov* 28:3, "He puts an end to darkness." Thus, He put an end to Yosef's term of imprisonment, and when the appointed time arrived, "Pharaoh dreamed."

In order to understand this *Midrash*, we must consider the universal rule that all events are governed by the law of cause and effect, but not always are the cause and the effect as they appear. For instance, if a merchant purchases a quantity of goods which he subsequently sells at a huge profit, then it would appear that the purchase of the goods are the cause which effected the profit. When we view the transaction from a Torah perspective, we arrive at a conclusion that is quite the opposite. We realize that Hashem had decreed this financial gain, and the acquisition of the merchandise is merely the conduit through which Hashem chooses to enrich the

[מא:א] ויהי מקץ שנתים ימים ופרעה חלם והנה עמד על היאר.

[41:1] **And it came to pass, at the end of two full years that Pharaoh dreamed, and behold, he stood by the river.**

TORAH TREASURES • *Mikaytz*

merchant. Thus, the predestined profit is the cause, and the purchase of the goods is the effect.

Similarly, in the case of Pharaoh's dreams, at first glance it would appear that Pharaoh's dreams were the cause that effected Yosef's release from prison. In reality, however, quite the opposite was true. The moment for Yosef's release had arrived, and this was the cause for Pharaoh's dreams. Thus, Yosef's release was the cause that had the effect of bringing about Pharaoh's dreams.

Bais Halevi

[מא:א] ויהי מקץ שנתים ימים ופרעה חלם והנה עמד על היאר.

[41:1] **And it came to pass, at the end of two full years that Pharaoh dreamed, and behold, he stood by the river.**

ויהי מקץ שנתים ימים ופרעה חלם . . .
And it came to pass, at the end of two full years that Pharaoh dreamed . . .

It is written (*Tehillim* 126:1), "When Hashem will return the captivity of Zion, we will be like dreamers." With the coming of *Mashiach*, when the world will be filled with understanding, we will realize then that all our mundane pleasures were nothing but an empty, fleeting dream. This concept can be homiletically derived from the abovementioned verse.

And it came to pass, at the end of two full years. A person awakens from his sleep (a play on words, *mikaytz shnassayim* becoming *maikitz mishnasso*), the sleep of his mundane life as he whiles away his days in futile and vain pursuits. *And Pharaoh dreamed.* Then he comes to the realization that his inner Pharaoh (the *yetzer hora*, also based on the root *pera*, meaning unruly or disorderly), his inner drive to break the rules, has no substance, no intrinsic value; it is but a dream. At last, he understands that the only true delight exists in clinging to Hashem.

Rabbi Zvi Yosef of Strettin

... ואין פותר אותם לפרעה
... and there was none that could interpret them to Pharaoh

Rashi explains that there were some magicians who did interpret the dreams, but not to Pharaoh's satisfaction.

Rabbeinu Efraim poses the following question: According to the well-known *Gemara* in *Berachos* 55b that dreams are fulfilled according to the interpretations of the interpreter, why didn't the magicians' interpretation come true?

It may be that this applies only when the interpretation convinces the dreamer as being plausible and well-founded, either for good or ill. Thus, the ominous interpretation of the baker's dream, sounding credible to him, came true. However, since Pharaoh had misgivings about the magicians' interpretations, their interpretations did not come true.

Chomas Anoch

[41:8] And it came to pass in the morning that his spirit was troubled, and he sent and called for all the magicians of Egypt and all its wise men, and Pharaoh told them his dream, and there was none that could interpret them to Pharaoh.

ויגלח ...
and he cut his hair ...

Rashi, quoting from *Beraishis Rabba*, explains that he did so in deference to the king. What is the relevance of this comment?

The *Gemara* in *Rosh Hashannah* teaches that Yosef was released from the dungeon on *Rosh Hashannah*. We also know that the *Avos* observed all the *mitzvos* of the Torah even before it was given. Accordingly, the question arises as to how Yosef could have cut his hair on *Yom Tov*? Responding to this question, Rashi emphasizes that he had no choice but to do so in deference to the king.

Chasam Sofer

[41:14] Then Pharaoh sent and called Yosef, and they rushed him from the dungeon, and he cut his hair and changed his clothes and went in to Pharaoh.

TORAH TREASURES • *Mikaytz*

ויגלח ...
and he cut his hair ...

Rashi, quoting from *Beraishis Rabba*, explains that he did so in deference to the king.

The significance of Rashi's comment may be traced to the *Gemara* in *Shabbos* 139, which expounds the verse in *Beraishis* 49:26, "And the crown of the head of the most abstentious of his brothers ..." From the time Yosef was separated from his brothers he did not taste wine. The *Halachah* states that anyone who, as a *nazir*, abstains from wine, must observe all the laws of *nezirus*. Thus, Yosef could not cut his hair; he only did so in deference to the king.

Devash Vechalav

[מא:כח] הוא הדבר אשר דברתי אל פרעה אשר האלקים עשה הראה את פרעה.

[41:28] "That is what I said to Pharaoh; what the Lord is about to do He has shown to Pharaoh."

... הראה את פרעה
... He has shown to Pharaoh

Everyone is pleased to be the bearer of glad tidings and to announce them in great detail, whereas the bearer of bad news confines himself to hints, gestures and grimaces.

In the same way, our Sages state that Hashem does not associate His Name with evil. Accordingly, interpreting the dream of the fat-fleshed cows, symbolizing the prosperous years, Yosef says: "What Hashem is about to do he has declared to Pharaoh." By contrast, regarding the dream of the lean cows, symbolizing the lean years, he states, "Hashem has shown to Pharaoh."

Rabbi Shlomo Kluger

[מא:מה] ויקרא פרעה שם יוסף צפנת פענח ויתן לו את אסנת בת פוטי פרע כהן אן לאשה ויצא

... את אסנת
Asenas ...

The numerical value of את אסנת, *Asenas*, is

equivalent to that of the words והיא בת דינה היתה, *and she was Dinah's daughter*. *Tzeidah Laderech*, citing this *Midrash*, provides the historical background for this *gematria*.

Asenas was indeed Dinah's daughter, fathered by Shechem. Yaakov made an amulet for her which he hung around her neck. When Asenas was taken from his house, she hid among the thorn bushes and the thistles. Her name, Asenas, was derived from the *sneh*, the bush behind which she hid. The angel Gavriel brought her to Egypt, where she was presented to the wife of Potifar, and because she was raised in Potifar's house she is spoken of as his daughter.

When Yosef went out over all Egypt, all the women came out to see his beauty and each one would throw a piece of jewelry at him in order to attract his attention (cf. Yonassan ben Uziel in *Beraishis* 49:22). Asenas tossed the amulet she was wearing around her neck. Yosef, realizing that she was Yaakov's granddaughter, married her.

Tzeidah Laderech

יוסף על ארץ מצרים.

[41:45] And Pharaoh called Yosef's name Tzafnas Pa'aneach, and he gave him as a wife Asenas the daughter of Potifera, priest of On. And Yosef went out to oversee the land of Egypt.

... כי נשני אלקים את כל עמלי
... because the Lord has made me forget my hardships

Ordinarily, the verse states clearly that the person giving the name expressed his reasons (see *Beraishis* 29:32). Thus, one would have expected the verse to read as follows: ... because *he said*, "the Lord had made me forget..." In this case, however, the verse gives the reason for the name but does not mention that Yosef expressed the reasons. This was because Pharaoh did not understand Hebrew, and Yosef had sworn not to reveal this.

[מא:נא-נב] ויקרא יוסף את שם הבכור מנשה כי נשני אלקים את כל עמלי ואת כל בית אבי. ואת שם השני קרא אפרים כי הפרני אלקים בארץ עניי.

[41:51-52] And Yosef named the firstborn Menesheh "because the Lord has made me forget my hardships and my father's household." And he named the second

Efraim "because the Lord has made me fruitful in the land of my affliction."

(*Gemara Sotah* 36b). Therefore, Yosef was unable to announce his reasons because doing so would have meant explaining the Hebrew meanings to Pharaoh. The Torah, however, does relate his unannounced reasons.

Meshech Chochmah

[מב:ב] ויאמר הנה שמעתי כי יש שבר במצרים רדו שמה ושברו לנו משם ונחיה ולא נמות.

[42:2] And he said: "Behold, I have heard that there is food in Egypt, go down there and buy for us from there that we may live and not die."

... ונחיה ולא נמות

... that we may live and not die

The root of the word ונחיה, *that we may live*, is *chaim*, which means life, but *chaim* has a dual connotation. In its rudimentary sense, *chaim* means the most basic form of life as opposed to death. Seen from a wider perspective, *chaim* can also denote the good life, the life of comfort and luxury.

Having always enjoyed a life of abundant prosperity in Yaakov's house, his sons might think their instructions were to buy enough food to live in the comfort to which they were accustomed. In order to avoid any misunderstanding, Yaakov stated his wish in the most unambiguous terms, "that we may live and not die." They were to buy this much and no more, for it is prohibited to live in luxury when the world is suffering famine.

Rabbi Naftoli Tzvi Yehudah Berlin

[מב:ט] ויזכר יוסף את החלמות אשר חלם להם ויאמר אלהם מרגלים אתם לראות את ערות הארץ באתם.

[42:9] Then Yosef remembered the dreams he had dreamed of them, and he said to them: "You

... ויאמר אלהם מרגלים אתם לראות את ערות הארץ באתם

... and he said to them: "You are spies! You have come to see the weakness of the land."

This accusation indicates a careful design and strategy on the part of Yosef. Had he charged them with any other crime they undoubtedly would have made inquiries about the identity of this unfair ruler who denounces innocent people. In the course of their inquiries, they would have learned about Pharaoh's dream and the events that evolved from them, and Yosef's true identity would undoubtedly have been revealed. By accusing them of spying, however, Yosef could rest assured that the brothers would ask no questions of anyone, for any such inquiries would only reinforce the accusation.

Minchah Belulah

על דבר הכסף השב באמתחתינו בתחלה אנחנו מובאים ...
Because of the matter of the money that was returned in our packs at the first time are we arrested ...

The *Gemara* in *Shabbos* 31a states that the first question a person is asked on his day of judgment is if he conducted his business affairs honestly. Did you trade truthfully all your life?

We can find an allusion to this *Gemara* in this verse which can also translated as "Money matters are the first issues raised with us."

Vilna Gaon

ויכינו את המנחה ... כי שמעו כי שם יאכלו לחם
And they prepared the present ... for they heard that they would eat bread there

The word מנחה, *present*, also denotes the afternoon prayer service. ויכינו את המנחה, *and they prepared the Minchah*, can thus also be rendered as *they prepared to say the Minchah prayers*, in compliance with the verse, "prepare to meet your Lord, O Yisrael." (*Amos* 4:12) They had heard that they would eat bread in Yosef's house, and according to *Halachah* it is forbidden to begin a meal close to the hour of

TORAH TREASURES • *Mikaytz*

Minchah; therefore, first they prayed.

Rabbi Vidal Tzarfati

[מג:כח] ויאמרו שלום לעבדך לאבינו עודנו חי ויקדו וישתחו.

[43:28] **And they said: "Our father, your servant, is well. He is still alive." And they bowed their heads and prostrated themselves.**

... לעבדך לאבינו

Our father, your servant . . .

Our Sages state (*Pirkei d'Rabbi Eliezer*, 3a) that the sons of Yaakov said to Yosef ten times: "Our father, your servant." Since Yosef allowed his father to be spoken of in such terms without objection, his life was shortened by ten years.

Upon scrutinizing the text, however, we find only five instances of Yaakov's sons mentioning the words "Our father, your servant."

This can be explained by turning to verse 42:23 where we read that "they knew not that Yosef understood them for the interpreter was between them." Consequently, Yosef heard the phrase "Our father, your servant" ten times, namely, five times from the brothers and five more times from the interpreter who translated their words.

Traditional

[מד:ה] הלוא זה אשר ישתה אדני בו והוא נחש ינחש בו הרעתם אשר עשיתם.

[44:5] **"It is the one from which my Lord drinks, and he uses it for divination. You have done an evil thing."**

... והוא נחש ינחש בו

. . . and he uses it for divination

That is to say that he, being a non-Jew, is allowed to practice divination, but you, to whom witchcraft is forbidden, have no practical use for the goblet. Therefore, taking it constituted a clear case of wanton theft, and "you have done an evil thing."

Keeping this in mind, we can justify the *kal vachomer* (a *fortiori* reasoning; deducing the rule for the major from the rule for the minor) the brothers employed in verse 44:8: "Behold, the money we found in the openings of our sacks we brought back to you . . . why then should we steal silver or gold from your lord's house?"

Obviously, their reasoning is open to question, for the goblet holds a much greater attraction than its silver and gold content; it is a priceless instrument with which the future can be foretold! Considering, however, that soothsaying is prohibited to the Jewish people, the magic powers of the goblet were worthless to them, and for them, its only value was indeed its silver and gold content. Thus, the logic of their *kal vachomer* reasoning was unassailable.

Nachal Kedumim

ויחפש בגדול החל ובקטן כלה . . .
And he searched, starting with the eldest and finishing with the youngest . . .

The *Midrash* tells us that the eldest in this verse was Shimon and the youngest was Binyamin. The question immediately arises: Wasn't Reuven the eldest son? The solution may be found in the brothers' statement upon being apprehended, ostensibly for having stolen the goblet.

They argued: "Behold, the money we found in our sacks' we brought back to you from the land of Canaan, why then should we steal silver or gold from your lord's house?" This argument was founded on purely rational *kal vachomer* reasoning (a *fortiori*; deducing the rule for the major from the rule for the minor), since Yosef's steward had not yet produced the goblet as evidence.

The steward now replied: "You make a compelling case, but not where Shimon and Binyamin are concerned, since Shimon was in

[מד:יב] ויחפש בגדול החל ובקטן כלה וימצא הגביע באמתחת בנימן.

[44:12] And he searched, starting with the eldest and finishing with the youngest, and the goblet was found in Binyamin's pack.

Egypt and Binyamin was not involved in the first incident at all. Therefore, they had no part in returning the money."

For this reason, he only searched the sacks of Shimon and Binyamin. Hence, the statement of the *Midrash* that the eldest was Shimon, this being because Reuven's sack was not searched.

Maharil Diskin

Allusions to Chanukah

... שבו שברו לנו מעט אכל

... Go again and buy us a little food

This verse alludes to the fact that the portion of *Mikaytz* is always read on *Chanukah*.

The numerical value of לנו, *for us*, equals 86. The root of the word שברו, *buy*, is שבר, *to break*. Thus, שברו לנו could be construed as break לנו, or break the number 86 in half, yielding 43. The words מעט אכל, *a little food*, could also be interpreted as the smallest letter (the letter with the smallest numerical value) in the word אכל, which is א, *aleph*, with a numerical value of 1. Hence, the entire phrase thus produces a total of 44.

[מג:ב] ויהי כאשר כלו לאכל את השבר אשר הביאו ממצרים ויאמר אליהם אביהם שבו שברו לנו מעט אכל.

[43:2] **And it came to pass when they had eaten up the food which they had brought out of Egypt, their father said to them: "Go again and buy us a little food."**

מקץ • TORAH TREASURES

Forty-four is exactly the combined total of all the *Chanukah* lights lit throughout the eight days of *Chanukah*, i.e. 36 lights plus 8 *shamashim* for a total of 44.

Otzar Chaim

... וטבח טבח והכן
... and have animals slaughtered and prepared

The *R'ma* in *Shulchan Aruch* (*Orech Chaim* 670) quotes some authorities who recommend an elaborate feast on *Chanukah* to commemorate the re-dedication of the altar.

The *Mordechai* finds an allusion to this custom in the verse וטבח טבח והכן, *and have animals slaughtered and prepared*. If we combine the letters in the word והכן with the last letter of the preceding word (the ח, *ches*, of טבח), we obtain the letters of the word חנוכה, *Chanukah*. This is a symbolic allusion to the custom of preparing a feast on *Chanukah*.

Otzar Chaim

At the conclusion of each weekly portion there is a listing of the number of verses of which it is composed. The sole exception is the portion of *Mikaytz*, which in addition to the number of verses also has a listing of the total number of words it contains, this total being 2,025. The Vilna Gaon offers the following explanation:

[מג:טז] וירא יוסף אתם את בנימין ויאמר לאשר על ביתו הבא את האנשים הביתה וטבח טבח והכן כי אתי יאכלו האנשים בצהרים.

[43:16] And Yosef saw Binyamin with them and he said to the overseer of his house: "Bring these men into the house, and have animals slaughtered and prepared, for the men shall dine with me at noon."

TORAH TREASURES • *Mikaytz*

> The portion of *Mikaytz* is always read on *Shabbos Chanukah*, and the 2025 words of which it is composed hint at this concurrence. The *gematria* for נר, *lamp*, amounts to 250. We then multiply this number by eight because there are eight days of *Chanukah*, and we arrive at 2000. Since we begin lighting candles on the 25th day of *Kislev*, we add an additional 25, resulting in a total of 2,025, thus establishing the connection between *Mikaytz* and *Chanukah*.
>
> *Otzar Chaim*

Vayigash / ויגש

ויגש אליו יהודה ויאמר בי אדני ...
And Yehudah approached him and said: "O my lord, let your servant, I pray you ...

The cantillation signs on these words are *kadma va'azla, revi'i, zarkah, munach* and *segol*. The Vilna Gaon, with his innovative method of exegesis, finds profound meaning in the arrangement of these signs.

Earlier, Yehudah, in requesting Yaakov's consent to take Binyamin to Egypt had declared (43:9): "If I do not bring him to you and set him before you, then I will have sinned against you forever," forever meaning the World to Come. (In other words, he swore to Yaakov that if he would not bring Binyamin back to him, he would forfeit his portion in the World to Come.)

This statement and its implications are alluded to by these cantillation signs: *Kadma* means to precede, *va'azla* means to go and *revi'i* means fourth. Yehudah, the fourth son, stepped forward to speak to Yosef, rather than Reuven who was the oldest. The can-

[מד:יח] ויגש אליו יהודה ויאמר בי אדני ידבר נא עבדך דבר באזני אדני ואל יחר אפך בעבדך כי כמוך כפרעה.

[44:18] And Yehudah approached him and said: "O my lord, let your servant, I pray you, speak a word in my lord's ear, and let not your anger burn against your servant, even though you are just like Pharaoh."

TORAH TREASURES • *Vayigash*

tillation signs continue: *Zarka* means to cast, *munach* means to rest and *segol* is an allusion to *Am Segulah*, the treasured nation. Thus the explanation: Because Yehudah cast away his share in the resting place of the World to Come together with the treasured nation; because he had cut himself off of his share in the World to Come if he did not bring back Binyamin, Yehudah was the one who stepped forward to speak for Binyamin.

Vilna Gaon

[מד:יח] ויגש אליו יהודה ויאמר בי אדני ידבר נא עבדך דבר באזני אדני ואל יחר אפך בעבדך כי כמוך כפרעה.

[44:18] **And Yehuda approached him and said: "Oh my lord, let your servant, I pray you, speak a word in my lord's ear, and let not your anger burn against your servant, even though you are just like Pharoah."**

. . . ואל יחר אפך
. . . and let not your anger burn

Rashi comments that this teaches us that he spoke harshly to him.

Initially, Yehudah thought that this misfortune, that they would now all become slaves, had befallen them in divine retribution, measure for measure, for their selling of Yosef into slavery. Therefore, he said very meekly (44:16): "What can we say to my lord? What can we say? And how can we justify ourselves? The Lord has found out the sin of your servants. Here we are, slaves to my lord." The sin of which he speaks is the selling of Yosef into slavery.

But seeing that Yosef was setting the rest of the brothers free, keeping in bondage only Binyamin who had not even participated in the selling of Yosef, Yehudah now understood clearly that this entire affair was not a penalty for the sin of selling Yosef. Rather, Binyamin's arrest was based on false charges. Therefore, he spoke harshly to him.

Alshich

... והורידו עבדיך את שיבת עבדך אבינו ביגון שאלה
... and your servants will have brought down the gray hairs of our father, your servant, with grief to the grave

The Rebbe of Kotzk wondered why Yehudah was distressed about Yaakov's reaction but did not express concern that Binyamin's children might die of grief. The Rebbe answered that a child does not grieve for his father as much as a father grieves for his child. Continued the Rebbe: "The same holds true for us. We do not share Hashem's anguish in the same measure that He shares in our sorrows."

Memayanos Hanetzach

... בהתודע יוסף אל אחיו
... when Yosef made himself known to his brothers

Rabbeinu Efraim writes: The letters of the word בהתודע, *when he made himself known*, can be rearranged to read העבדות, *the slavery*. This explains why Yosef ordered all bystanders to leave. He did not want the Egyptians to hear his brothers' shame of having sold him into slavery.

Nachal Kedumim

ויאמר יוסף אל אחיו אני יוסף העוד אבי חי ולא יכלו אחיו לענות אתו כי נבהלו מפניו
And Yosef said to his brothers: "I am Yosef. Is my father still alive?" And his brothers could not answer him, because they were dismayed before him.

The *Midrash*, on this verse, quotes Abba Kohain Bardela: "Beware the Day of Judgment. Beware the Day of Rebuke. If Yosef's brothers couldn't withstand Yosef's rebuke,

[מד:לא] והיה כראותו כי אין הנער ומת והורידו עבדיך את שיבת עבדך אבינו ביגון שאלה.

[44:31] "So it will be, when he sees the lad is not there, he will die, and your servants will have brought down the gray hairs of our father, your servant, with grief to the grave."

[מה:א] ולא יכל יוסף להתאפק לכל הנצבים עליו ויקרא הוציאו כל איש מעלי ולא עמד איש אתו בהתודע יוסף אל אחיו.

[45:1] Then Yosef could no longer restrain himself for all those that stood by him and he called out: "Make every man leave my presence." And no man remained with him when Yosef made himself known to his brothers.

[מה:ג] ויאמר יוסף אל אחיו אני יוסף העוד אבי חי ולא יכלו אחיו לענות אתו כי נבהלו מפניו.

[45:3] And Yosef said to his brothers: "I am Yosef. Is my father still alive?" And his brothers could not answer him, because they were dismayed before him."

TORAH TREASURES • *Vayigash*

[מה:ג] ויאמר יוסף אל
אחיו אני יוסף העוד אבי
חי ולא יכלו אחיו לענות
אתו כי נבהלו מפניו.

[45:3] **And Yosef said to his brothers: "I am Yosef. Is my father still alive?" And his brothers could not answer him, because they were dismayed before him."**

how will it be when the Holy Blessed One comes to rebuke every individual according to what he is?"

The question arises: Where does the *Midrash* find a note of rebuke in Yosef's words to his brothers?

The Hebrew word for rebuke is תוכחה, a variation of the word הוכחה, proof or demonstration. Thus, the essence of rebuke is demonstration. By demonstrating to a person the full impact of his deeds, and the folly of his excuses, he can be brought to the realization that he has erred.

Yosef's words contained such a demonstration; he used their own words to demonstrate their guilt to them. Yehudah had approached the Viceroy of Egypt, unaware that he was Yosef, and pleaded for Binyamin's release for the sake of his old father who could not bear the loss of a young son. "I am Yosef," Yosef responded. As if to say: I am the Yosef whom you sold into slavery. "Is my father still alive?" As if to say: Was he able to bear the pain when you tore me from him? Why didn't you worry then about your father's pain, as you worry now?

It is no wonder, then, that the brothers were dismayed by Yosef's words. Their own words had been turned against them. The rebuke was clear. They had nothing to say.

This is also how it will be on the Day of Judgment. It will be a Day of Rebuke. Everyone's guilt will be demonstrated to him through his own deeds and words. What will he say? That he couldn't give *tzedakah* because he didn't have enough money? Then how did he find the money for all sorts of luxuries and pleasures? In this manner, everyone will be shown the folly of his ways, through his own deeds and words. And it will be impossible to offer an excuse.

Bais Halevi

וישלחני אלקים לפניכם לשום לכם שארית בארץ ולהחיות לכם לפליטה גדלה
And the Lord sent me before you to prepare for you a remnant in the land and to keep you alive for a great deliverance

The essence of Yosef's words is that sending him to Egypt was Hashem's master plan, in order for him to lay the groundwork for the eventual arrival of Yaakov and his sons.

The actualization of this arrival in Egypt is described in *Shemos* 1:1: "And these are the names of the sons of Yisrael who came into Egypt, every man came with his household."

The two verses thus complement each other, the events described in the former being the precursor and preparation to those in the latter. Now, let us compare the numerical value of these two verses. Most astonishingly, the intimate relationship of the two verses comes to the fore in their respective numerical values, which are identical—both mounting up to 3161! Thus, the *gematria* supports the historical relationship of the two passages.

Otzar Chaim

וישבת בארץ גשן והיית קרוב אלי . . .
And you shall dwell in the land of Goshen, and you shall be near to me . . .

On the surface, this seems to be a paradoxical statement. If he dwells in the land of Goshen which is outside of Egypt, he cannot be near Yosef who is in Egypt. Rabbi Meir of

TORAH TREASURES • *Vayigash*

me, you and your children and your grandchildren and your flocks and your herds and all that you possess."

Premyshlan offers this penetrating insight:

Often a little distance between friends causes true affection to thrive and grow all the more. That is what Yosef meant "if you shall dwell in the land of Goshen," especially then, "you shall feel close to me."

Daas Chachamim

[מה:כב] לכלם נתן לאיש חלפות שמלת ולבנימן נתן שלש מאות כסף וחמש חלפת שמלת.

[45:22] **He gave each of them a set of garments, and to Binyamin he gave three hundred shekels of silver and five sets of garments.**

... ולבנימן נתן שלש מאות כסף

... and to Binyamin he gave three hundred shekels of silver

The motive for giving Binyamin three hundred shekels may be attributed to the *Halachah* that anyone selling his slave to a non-Jew (thereby preventing him from fulfilling his *mitzvah* obligations) is fined an amount of up to ten times the value of the slave. Inasmuch as the standard value of a slave is valued at thirty shekels, the resulting fine would be three hundred shekels.

Yosef did not give money to any of his brothers except for Binyamin who had not taken part in selling him into slavery. Thus, by withholding the 300 shekels from his brothers that he did give Binyamin, Yosef was, in effect, penalizing each one of them 300 shekels.

Mahara of Worms

... ולבנימן נתן שלש מאות כסף וחמש חלפת שמלת

... and to Binyamin he gave three hundred shekels of silver and five sets of garments

It is interesting to note that the word חלפות, *garments*, appears twice in this verse, each time spelled differently. The first time it appears in its full form, with a ו, *vav*, the second time in its abbreviated form, without a *vav*.

This anomaly can be explained according to

the statement of Rashi in *Devarim* 9:11 that a pluralized word spelled in the abbreviated form (which resembles the singular) indicates that both items are identical. Thus, since the brothers were not identical in size, and consequently, the garments given to them were also not identical, the full form of the word is used. However, the five garments given to Binyamin were identical, since they were all made for the same person. Therefore, the word appears in its abbreviated form.

Rabbi Chaim Berlin

... And he offered sacrifices to the Lord of his father Yitzchak

Our Rabbis state that Yaakov was chastised for not honoring his father during the twenty-two years that he spent in Charan. His retribution was the twenty-two years of agonizing over Yosef. This observation prompts us to wonder: We know that a father can legally overlook the honor that is due him and that in such a case the son is absolved from honoring his father. Surely, Yitzchak must have forgiven Yaakov for his involuntary omission of this *mitzvah*. The answer is as follows:

The failure to honor one's father involves two aspects, the lack of fulfillment of one's obligations towards one's father and the lack of fulfillment of Hashem's command to honor one's father. Yitzchak, did indeed, overlook his part of the *mitzvah*, but Hashem's part was not forgiven. In fact, Hashem deals very strictly with those closest to him, and thus Yaakov was punished because of Hashem's part of the *mitzvah*.

Thus, when the twenty-two years of agony

[מו:א] ויסע ישראל וכל אשר לו ויבא בארה שבע ויזבח זבחים לאלקי אביו יצחק.

[46:1] **And Yisrael journeyed with all his possessions, and he came to Be'er Sheva, and he offered sacrifices to the Lord of his father Yitzchak.**

were completed, he offered sacrifices to "the Lord of his father Yitzchak", for he had transgressed only against Hashem. This also explains why the Torah writes "the Lord of Yitzchak" and not "the Lord of Avraham."

Chomas Anoch

[כט: מו] ויאסר יוסף מרכבתו ויעל לקראת ישראל אביו גשנה וירא אליו ויפל על צואריו ויבך על צואריו עוד.

[46:29] And Yosef harnessed up his chariot and went up to meet his father Yaakov, to Goshen, and presented himself to him, and he fell upon his shoulders, and he wept long upon his shoulders.

... ויפל על צואריו ויבך על צואריו עוד

... and he fell upon his shoulders, and he wept long upon his shoulders

Rashi comments that it was Yosef who did all these things, but Yaakov did not fall upon his shoulders or kiss him. Instead, he recited the *Shema*. The question arises: If there existed at that moment the obligation of reading the *Shema*, why didn't Yosef also recite it? The Maharal of Prague in *Gur Aryeh* advances an illuminating explanation.

Actually, he states, it was not the time of reciting the *Shema* at all, but it is the way of righteous men that in times of great joy their hearts are filled with a burning desire to be joined with the Creator and to proclaim His Oneness with love for having showered His goodness on them. Thus, upon meeting Yosef after this long separation, Yaakov felt the urge to recite the *Shema*, thereby declaring Hashem's Oneness, and accepting upon himself the yoke of heavenly sovereignty with joy and love.

Yosef, on the other hand, could not recite the *Shema*, since he had the duty to fulfill the *mitzvah* of honoring his father and could not interrupt it for a non-obligatory reading of the *Shema*. Acts performed above and beyond the strict requirements of law (*lifnim meshuras hadin*) are acceptable to Hashem only if all the requirements of the law have been fulfilled. In the words of *Chovos Halevovos*: "An addition is desirable only if the main object remains intact."

Birkas Peretz

Author's note:
According to the Maharal's explanation, the argument could be made that the meeting did occur at the time designated for reading *Shema*, but specifically at the very beginning of that time period. Therefore, Yaakov who was not occupied with another *mitzvah* was eager to read it at once, since "the zealous perform the *mitzvos* at the earliest time." (*Pesachim* 71b; cf. *Orach Chaim* 58:2: "It is recommended to recite the *Shema* at the earliest possible time.") But Yosef, being engaged in the *mitzvah* of honoring his father, waited until later to recite the *Shema*.

. . . לחם לפי הטף
. . . with bread, even to the littlest ones

It was within Yosef's power to provide them with the finest delicacies fit for a king. Yet, he only "sustained them with bread." Why? Because, as it is stated in the next verse (47:13): "And there was no bread in the land." In times of famine, even a king and his household are forbidden to say: "I shall eat, drink and all will be well with me."

Siporno

Author's note:
On the same topic, we quoted the comments of Rabbi Naftoli Tzvi Yehudah Berlin (the *Netziv*) on verse 42:2.

[מז:יב] ויכלכל יוסף את אביו ואת אחיו ואת כל בית אביו לחם לפי הטף.

[47:12] **And Yosef sustained his father and his brothers and all his father's household with bread, even to the littlest ones.**

Vayechi / ויחי

ושכבתי עם אבתי ...
And I will lie down to sleep with my fathers ...
By equating death with sleep, this verse corroborates the principle of *techiyas hamaysim*, the resurrection of the dead; the expression "going to sleep" carries the distinct suggestion of eventual arising. Only in the context of a curse is it written (*Tehillim* 41:9): "And now that he lies down to sleep, he shall rise up no more." The clear implication, however, is that in general, sleep is followed by arising.

Me'or Einayim

[מז:ל] ושכבתי עם אבתי ונשאתני ממצרים וקברתני בקברתם ויאמר אנכי אעשה כדברך.

[47:30] And I will lie down to sleep with my fathers, and carry me out of Egypt and bury me in their burying place. And he said, "I will do as you have said."

ויאמר ליוסף הנה אביך חלה ...
And one said to Yosef: "Behold, your father is sick ..."
The *Gemara* tells us (*Bava Metzia* 87a) that until Yaakov there was no illness, since Yaakov is the first mentioned to have been ill. Then Yaakov came and prayed and illness came into being, as it is written: "One said to Yosef, 'Behold, your father is sick.'"

[מח:א] ויהי אחרי הדברים האלה ויאמר ליוסף הנה אביך חלה ויקח את שני בניו עמו את מנשה ואת אפרים.

[48:1] And it came to pass after these things that one said to Yosef: "Behold, your father is sick." And he took with him

TORAH TREASURES • *Vayechi*

his two sons Menasheh and Efraim.

This *Gemara* apparently contradicts a statement of the *Gemara* in *Sotah* 14 which states that Hashem appeared to Avraham (*Beraishis* 18:1) in order to visit the sick, this being the source for the *mitzvah* of *bikur cholim*, visiting the sick. Evidently, there was sickness even before Yaakov. The identical question is raised by *Tosefos* regarding a statement of the *Gemara* in *Bava Basra* 26: "A jeweled pendant was hanging from Avraham's neck. Any sick person gazing upon it was healed instantly." Apparently, there was sickness before Yaakov.

Tosefos resolves the difficulty by suggesting that these were illnesses caused by an inflicted wound, as for example Avraham's illness which resulted from his circumcision. As an alternate answer, *Tosefos* suggests that until Yaakov there were indeed diseases, but there were no life-threatening diseases.

Iturei Torah

[מח:ב] ויגד ליעקב
ויאמר הנה בנך יוסף בא
אליך ויתחזק ישראל
וישב על המטה.

[48:2] And one told Yaakov and said: "Behold, your son Yosef comes to you." And Yisrael strengthened himself and sat on the bed.

... המטה

... the bed

The numerical value of the word המטה, *the bed*, equals 59. This is particularly interesting in light of the *Gemara* in *Nedarim* 39 which states that anyone visiting a sick person takes away one sixtieth of his illness.

Thus, the verse is saying that Yosef had come to visit Yaakov on his sickbed and took away one sixtieth of his illness. This can also be homiletically interpreted as the meaning of "he strengthened himself and sat על המטה, *on the bed*," meaning he gained new strength because 59 parts remained of his illness, one sixtieth having been taken away by Yosef's visit.

Otzar Chaim

ויחי • TORAH TREASURES

... אפרים ומנשה כראובן ושמעון יהיו לי
... Efraim and Menasheh, as Reuven and Shimon, shall be mine

The numerical value of אפרים ומנשה, *Efraim and Menasheh*, is 732. It is equivalent to that of ראובן ושמעון, *Reuven and Shimon*, which is 731, plus the *kollel*, the additional 1, equals the totality of the entire term.

In fact, this verse is the prime source for the rule that in the computation of *gematria* it is permissible to add the *kollel* of 1 to one of the values in order to achieve the equation.

Bnei Yisaschar

... האלקים הרעה אתי מעודי עד היום הזה
... the Lord Who has been my shepherd all my life long until this day

The numerical value of מעודי, *all my life long*, equals 130, which represents Yaakov's age at the time of his arrival in Egypt. The *gematria* of הזה, *this*, equals 17, representing the 17 years he lived in Egypt.

Otzar Chaim

האספו ...
Gather together ...

The exile in Egypt, their first exile, evolved from the quarreling and discord between Yosef and his brothers. Later on in history, the destruction of the *Bais Hamikdash* and the subsequent exile were brought about by *sin'as chinam*, unwarranted hatred between fellow Jews.

Yaakov, in his prophetic vision, entreated his sons to "gather together," to live together in harmony and not to be torn by conflict and dissension. Only thus will you diminish the

[מח:ה] ועתה שני בניך הנולדים לך בארץ מצרים עד באי אליך מצרימה לי הם אפרים ומנשה כראובן ושמעון יהיו לי.

[48:5] And now, your two sons who were born to you in the land of Egypt before I came to you into Egypt are mine; Efraim and Menasheh, as Reuven and Shimon, shall be mine.

[מח:טו] ויברך את יוסף ויאמר האלקים אשר התהלכו אבתי לפניו אברהם ויצחק האלקים הרעה אתי מעודי עד היום הזה.

[48:15] And he blessed Yosef and said: "The Lord before Whom my fathers Avraham and Yitzchak did walk, the Lord Who has been my shepherd all my life long until this day."

[מט:א] ויקרא יעקב אל בניו ויאמר האספו ואגידה לכם את אשר יקרא אתכם באחרית הימים.

[49:1] And Yaakov called his sons and said: "Gather together, that I may tell you what shall befall you in the end of days."

TORAH TREASURES • *Vayechi*

danger of "what shall befall you in the end of days."

Ahavas Yonasan

את אשר יקרא אתכם באחרית הימים ...
... what shall befall you in the end of days

The word יקרא, *befall*, has the connotation of a random occurrence. Every Jew will be engaged in his business and preoccupied with his work when suddenly, *Mashiach* will appear, totally unexpected; everyone will be caught by surprise.

Baal Shem Tov

[מט:ג] ראובן בכרי אתה
כחי וראשית אוני יתר
שאת ויתר עז.

[49:3] "Reuven, you are my firstborn, my strength and the first fruit of my manhood, greatest in rank and greatest in power."

... ראובן בכרי אתה
Reuven, you are my firstborn ...

Concealed in these verses is a truly astonishing *gematria*. The addition of the values of the first letters of the words following the names in each blessing yields the sum total of 365, the number of days in the solar year. Furthermore, by adding the last letters in each blessing, the number 354 is obtained, the number of days in the lunar year.

This *gematria* is in line with the ideas expressed in the following verses (*Yirmiyah* 31:35-36): "Thus says Hashem, who gives the sun for a light by day, and the ordinances of the moon and the stars for a light by night... If these ordinances depart from before Me, says Hashem, then the offspring of Yisrael shall also cease from being a nation before Me forever." The underlying meaning of Yirmiyah's words is that just as these cosmic laws will never cease so the nation of Israel shall endure forever.

Baal Haturim

יהודה אתה יודוך אחיך ...
Yehudah, your brothers shall praise you ...

It is noteworthy that in Yehudah's blessing all the letters of the Hebrew alphabet can be found, with the exception of the letter ז, *zayin*, which does not appear. The omission of this letter alludes to the fact that *Mashiach*, who will be a direct descendant of Yehudah, will not achieve victory by force of arms. (*Zayin*, in addition to being the seventh letter of the Hebrew alphabet, also means weapons or arms.) Rather, his ascendancy will come about instantaneously, solely through divine intervention.

Rabbeinu Bachya

[מט:ח] יהודה אתה יודוך אחיך ידך בערף איביך ישתחוו לך בני אביך.

[49:8-12] "Yehudah, your brothers shall praise you; your hand shall be upon the nape of your enemies; your father's sons shall bow down before you."

... ידך בערף איביך ישתחוו לך בני אביך
... your hand shall be upon the nape of your enemies; your father's sons shall bow down before you

When King Shaul, at the behest of Shmuel Hanavi, proceeded to carry out the *mitzvah* of annihilating Amalek, it is written (*Shmuel I* 15:4): "And Shaul summoned the people and counted them in Tela'im, two hundred thousand footmen, and ten thousand men of Yehudah." The text differentiates between the "people" and the "men of Yehudah." When they returned from the battle, bringing with them a rich booty of "the best of the sheep and the oxen," thereby violating Hashem's command, Shaul explained to Shmuel "for the people spared the best of the sheep and of the oxen." (*Shmuel I* 15:15) The inference is that only "the people" sinned by sparing the sheep and oxen, but that the ten thousand "men of Yehudah" utterly destroyed all of Amalek's possessions in total compliance with Hashem's command.

TORAH TREASURES • *Vayechi*

For not participating in the sinful action of "the people", the tribe of Yehudah earned the monarchy. As a result of this sin, King Shaul lost his throne, and David, who belonged to the tribe of Yehudah, succeeded him.

This is implied in the words: "Your hands shall be upon the nape of your enemies," meaning, because you totally subdued and eradicated your enemy Amalek, not showing him any mercy, therefore "your father's sons shall bow down before you." In other words, you will earn the crown of royalty.

Meshech Chochmah

[מט:טו] וירא מנחה כי טוב ואת הארץ כי נעמה ויט שכמו לסבל ויהי למס עבד.

[49:15] "For he saw that the resting place was good and the land was pleasant, and he bowed his shoulder to burden and became a servant under taskwork."

וירא מנחה כי טוב . . . ויט שכמו לסבל
For he saw that the resting place was good . . . and he bowed his shoulder to burden

If a person wishes to live a life of tranquility, he must accustom himself to endure with equanimity any misfortune that may come his way, any pain his fellow-man may inflict on him. Only then will he live in serene calmness.

Rabbi Bunim of Pshischa

. . . ויט שכמו לסבל
. . . and he bowed his shoulder to burden

The fast of the Tenth of *Teves* occurs during the week in which the portion of *Vayechi* is read. An allusion to this fast-day can be found in the words ויט שכמו לסבל, *and he bowed his shoulder to burden*. The word יט represents the initials of י' טבת, *the Tenth of Teves*.

Otzar Chaim

. . . דן ידין עמו
Dan shall judge his people . . .

ויחי • TORAH TREASURES

There is a popular custom of reading the *Parshas Hanesi'im*, the portion of the Princes, on the twelve day period beginning with Rosh Chodesh Nissan until the twelfth day of Nissan, one *nasi* each day.

This portion, which appears in *Naso* (*Bamidbar* 7), describes the individual offering each of the princes of the twelve tribes brought at the dedication of the altar, which occurred during these twelve days of *Nissan*.

A closer analysis reveals the fact that the day of the week on which the segment of the *nasi* of Dan is read is always the day on which the first day of the following *Rosh Hashannah* will fall. For example, if the segment of the *nasi* of Dan is read on a Tuesday, then the first day of the following *Rosh Hashannah* will also occur on Tuesday.

Our verse (49:16) contains an amazing allusion to this calendrical coincidence. דן ידין עמו, *Dan shall judge his people*, can also be read as: On the day we read the portion of the *nasi* of Dan, on that very same day will Hashem sit in judgment on His people, namely on *Rosh Hashannah*.

Rabbi Shlomo Zalman Volozhiner

[מט:טז] דן ידין עמו
כאחד שבטי ישראל.

[49:16] "Dan shall judge his people, as one of the tribes of Yisrael."

עלי עין . . .
by a fountain . . .

The letters in the aleph-bais that come after the letters עין, *fountain*, are the following: ע, *ayin*, is followed by פ, *peh*; י, *yud*, is followed by כ, *kaff*; נ, *nun*, is followed by ס, *samach*. By rearranging the order of these three letters, the word כסף, *money*, is obtained. This is an allusion to the moral lesson that by giving charity one is protected from death and from *ayin hora*, the evil eye.

[מט:כב] בן פרת יוסף בן
פרת עלי עין בנות צעדה
עלי שור.

[49:22] "Yosef is a fruitful vine, a fruitful vine by a fountain, its branches running over the wall."

TORAH TREASURES • *Vayechi*

[מט:ח] יהודה אתה
יודוך אחיך ידך בערף
איביך ישתחוו לך בני
אביך.

[49:8-12] "Yehudah, your brothers shall praise you; your hand shall be upon the nape of your enemies; your father's sons shall bow down before you."

This thought is expressed in the words עלי עין, *by a fountain*. Literally translated, this means above *ayin*, meaning the letters that are above or following the letters of the word *ayin*, will protect him from *ayin hora*.

Continuing in this vein, we note that the letters following כסף form the word עצל, *lazy, laggard*. This expresses the thought that whoever delays giving charity is in violation of *bal te'acher*, as expressed by the verse in *Devarim* 23:22, "Do not be slack to pay your vow."

Nachal Kedumim

Torah Treasures

Shemos / שמות

Shemos / שמות

ואלה שמות בני ישראל הבאים מצרימה . . .
And these are the names of the people of Yisrael who came into Egypt . . .

The last letters of the words ואלה שמות בני ישראל הבאים, if rearranged, combine to form the word תהלים, *Tehillim*. The word following this phrase is מצרימה, *to Egypt,* which may be considered as a modification of the root מיצר, *straits, distress.* The juxtaposition of these two words teaches us that the recitation of *Tehillim* will help us in times of distress.

Yechahein Pe'eir

[א:א] ואלה שמות בני ישראל הבאים מצרימה את יעקב איש וביתו באו.

[1:1] **And these are the names of the people of Yisrael who came into Egypt with Yaakov, every man came with his household.**

ואלה שמות . . .
And these are the names . . .

The words ואלה שמות, *and these are the names,* the first two words of the book of *Shemos,* form an acronym consisting of the first letters of the words in the following sentence: וחייב אדם לקרות הפרשה שנים מקרא ואחד תרגום *Every Jew must read the weekly Torah portion, twice in the Hebrew text and once with*

Targum Onkelos, its Aramaic translation.

Chomas Anoch

Author's note:
This acronym may have a deeper meaning. Since the people of Yisrael were about to begin their life in exile, they would eventually forget the holy tongue to the extent that a translation would be needed. Thus, the verse which introduces the story of Yisrael's exile warns (through this acronym) that reading from the Torah in its original text will not be sufficient; a translation will also be needed.

[א:י] הבה נתחכמה לו פן ירבה והיה כי תקראנה מלחמה ונוסף גם הוא על שנאינו ונלחם בנו ועלה מן הארץ.

[1:10] Come, let us deal wisely with them, lest they multiply, and if we are faced by war, they too will join our enemies and do battle with us, driving us from the land.

הבה נתחכמה לו . . .
Come, let us deal wisely with them . . .

The *Gemara* in *Sotah* 11 relates that Pharaoh consulted with three advisors about which measures to take to repress the people of Yisrael. These three were Bilam, Iyov and Yisro.

Bilam gave malevolent advice; he was subsequently killed. Iyov remained silent; he was punished with pain and suffering. Yisro fled; he merited that his descendants would sit as judges in the Chamber of the Great Sanhedrin.

The question arises: If Iyov offered no advice, why was he punished with pain and suffering? Upon reflection, however, it becomes evident that Hashem's retribution was visited on him fairly, measure for measure.

Why, indeed, did Iyov remain silent at that moment? Obviously, he reasoned that any indignant outcry on his part would serve no purpose. Why raise a protest in vain? In order to show him the error of his thinking, Hashem's punishment took the form of physical suffering. Hashem wanted to demonstrate to Iyov that when in pain he would cry out, moan and groan, knowing full well that his wailing would not relieve his pain. Crying is a basic human reaction to pain. If Iyov would have been affected by the suffering of the Jewish people he would have cried out. Thus, his silence was an indication of his indifference and lack of compassion.

Rabbi Yitzchak Zev Soloveitchik

הבה נתחכמה לו פן ירבה . . .
Come, let us deal wisely with them, lest they multiply . . .

Rashi, quoting the *Midrash*, explains that in contrast to Pharaoh's words "lest they multiply," Hashem declared (*Shemos* 1:12), "the more they multiplied and the more they spread out." The intent of Pharaoh's decree of "lest they multiply" was the nullification of the divine mandate of "be fruitful and multiply."

It is interesting to note that the numerical value of the words הבה נתחכמה לו פן ירבה, *Come, let us deal wisely with them, lest they multiply*, equals 918. Surprisingly, 918 is also the numerical value of the verse in *Beraishis* 1:28: ויאמר להם אלקים פרו ורבו *And the Lord said to them, "Be fruitful and multiply."*

It was schemes such as Pharaoh's to which Shlomo Hamelech alluded in *Mishlei* 19:21: "There are many devices in a man's heart, but the counsel of Hashem shall stand."

Otzar Chaim

וימררו את חייהם . . .
And they embittered their lives . . .

The cantillation marks on these words allude to the answer to one of the difficult questions regarding *Yetzias Mitzraim*, the Exodus

TORAH TREASURES • *Shemos*

bittered their lives with hard labor, in mortar, brick and all manner of heavy field work, all their labors they made them perform were backbreaking.

of the Jewish people from Egypt.

Avraham had been told that his children would dwell in exile for 400 years, yet the Torah teaches us that Yisrael's sojourn in Egypt lasted only 210 years.

Our Sages explain the discrepancy by telling us that the extreme affliction and bitterness of Egyptian bondage made the 210 years as difficult as 400 years of more moderate exile.

The cantillation marks are *kadma va'azla*, which translates to "it hurried and went," or "it went before its time." By placing these cantillation marks upon the words "they embittered their lives," the Torah implies that the extreme embitterment of their lives was the reason that they "went before the time" of the completion of the predestined 400 years of bondage.

Vilna Gaon

[א:טז] ויאמר בילדכן את העבריות וראיתן על האבנים אם בן הוא והמתן אתו ואם בת היא וחיה.

[1:16] And he said: "When you deliver the Hebrew women, you shall look upon the birthstool; if it be a son, you shall put him to death, but if it is a daughter, she shall live."

... וראיתן על האבנים

... you shall look upon the birthstool

According to a *Massorah*, there are three verses, all containing the words וראיתם, *you shall look upon*, which are interconnected through their underlying meaning. Besides in the abovementioned verse, this word also appears in "And you shall look upon the land" (*Bamidbar* 13:18) and in "And you shall look upon it" (*ibid.* 15:39), referring to the *tzitzis*, which are meant to remind one of the *mitzvos* of Hashem.

In order to detect the common thread that ties these phrases together, we must focus on a *Mishnah* in *Pirkei Avos* (3:1): Know from where you have come, to where you are going and before Whom you will be brought for judgment and reckoning. From where you have come? From a putrid droplet. To where you are going? To a place of dust, worms and maggots. Before Whom you will be brought for judgment and reckoning? Before the King Who reigns over kings, the Holy One, Blessed be He.

The three phrases mentioned in the *Massorah* run parallel to the three questions in this *Mishnah*. "You shall look upon the birthstool" corresponds to knowing one's origin. "And you shall look upon the land" corresponds to knowing one's ultimate destiny. "And you shall look upon it" corresponds to knowing before Whom one will be brought for judgment and reckonings, both pertaining to Hashem, the Creator and Judge of the Universe.

Chidushei Mahari

ותקח לו תבת גמא . . . ותשם בסוף על שפת היאר
She took for him an ark of bulrushes . . . and placed it among the reeds by the riverbank

One may wonder: Could Hashem not have found a better way of rescuing the future savior of the Jewish people from Pharaoh's murderous decree than by having him cast into the river, as were all other Jewish boys?

No, even though he was the redeemer of Yisrael, he was not to be an exception. He, too, had to experience the cruel fate all Jewish boys had to endure.

Otzar Chaim

. . . כי המקום אשר אתה עומד עליו אדמת קדש הוא
. . . for the place where you stand is holy ground

People often say: "If I were not so preoccupied with my business affairs and plagued

[3:5] **And He said: "Come no closer. Remove your shoes from your feet, for the place where you stand is holy ground."**

with personal problems, I would be able to serve Hashem with greater dedication and piety."

The *Mishnah* in *Pirkei Avos* (2:5) provides a fitting response to this kind of wishful thinking: "Do not say when I have the opportunity I will study, for perhaps you will not have the opportunity."

Rabbi Simchah Bunim of Pshischa suggests that it is Hashem's Will that you serve Him under these less favorable circumstances. The Chafetz Chaim explains the abovementioned verse in a similar vein.

"For the place where you stand is holy ground." The precise situation in which you find yourself at this very moment is holy. Hashem expects you to serve Him in your situation and environment, despite the difficulties involved.

Panim Yafos

[ד:יא] ויאמר ה' אליו מי שם פה לאדם או מי ישום אלם או חרש או פקח או עור הלא אנכי ה'.

[4:11] **And Hashem said to him: "Who has made man's mouth, or who makes man mute or deaf or clear-sighted or blind? Is it not I, Hashem?"**

. . . אלם או חרש או פקח או עור

. . . mute or deaf or clear-sighted or blind

The question arises: Why does the Torah list the clear-sighted among the roster of the physically impaired? It is in order to remind every whole and healthy person that he too has many blemishes, faults and imperfections.

Baal Shem Tov

[ד:כב] ואמרת אל פרעה כה אמר ה' בני בכרי ישראל.

[4:22] **"And you shall say to Pharaoh: Thus says Hashem, Yisrael is My son, My firstborn."**

. . . בני בכרי ישראל

. . . Yisrael is My son, My firstborn

Why is Yisrael referred to as Hashem's firstborn? Certainly from a chronological perspective there would not seem to be any basis for such a title. The Torah records the name of many great and mighty nations that existed long before the emergence of Yisrael.

The outstanding feature, however, of a firstborn is that by virtue of his birth he bestows fatherhood on his father, allowing him use of the title "father."

Similarly, by declaring to the Universe the Sovereignty of Hashem as the sole Creator and Master of all destiny, Yisrael caused Hashem to be recognized as the Father, the Prime Cause of all Creation, in effect performing the function of the firstborn.

Meshech Chochmah

לא תאספון לתת תבן . . .
You shall no longer give the people straw . . .

This verse gives rise to a question. Inasmuch as Pharaoh wanted to increase the burden of labor on the Jewish people, why did he not continue to supply the straw while doubling their required production quota of bricks? Wasn't compelling them to gather straw comparatively light work?

This teaches us that mental strain and anxiety (as those associated with finding sufficient straw) are more crushing and exhausting than the most strenuous and oppressive physical toil.

Rabbi Yitzchok of Vorki

[ה:ז] לא תאספון לתת תבן לעם ללבן הלבנים כתמול שלשם הם ילכו וקששו להם תבן.

[5:7] "You shall no longer give the people straw to make brick, as in the past; let them go and gather straw for themselves."

תבן אין נתן לעבדיך ולבנים אמרים לנו עשו . . .
No straw is given to your servants, yet they say to us: 'Make bricks' . . .

The following is a beautiful example of the method of playing on words employed by many Chassidic greats. On the surface, these puns have the appearance of mere clever witticisms, but in reality, they are vehicles for the

[ה:טז] תבן אין נתן לעבדיך ולבנים אמרים לנו עשו והנה עבדיך מכים וחטאת עמך.

[5:16] "No straw is given to your servants, yet they say to us: 'Make bricks'; and, behold, your ser-

TORAH TREASURES • *Shemos*

vants are beaten, but your nation is guilty."

expression of profound truths. Rabbi Meir of Premyshlan, in his later years, once was sitting engrossed in thought. He stroked his flowing white beard and *peyos*, sighed sorrowfully and said:

"תבן אין נתן לעבדיך (using the word תבן as a form of the verb בינה, *understanding*). In our young years, we do not have the תבן, the wisdom to repent for our sins. However, לבנים (from the word לבן, *white*), the white hair of our beards, אמרים לנו, *tell us*, עשו, *do teshuvah*, repent before it is too late."

Rabbi Meir of Premyshlan

[א:ו] ויאמר ה' אל משה עתה תראה אשר אעשה לפרעה כי ביד חזקה ישלחם וביד חזקה יגרשם מארצו.

[6:1] **And Hashem said to Moshe: "Now you shall see what I will do to Pharaoh, for by a strong hand shall he let them go, and by a strong hand shall be drive them from his land."**

עתה תראה אשר אעשה לפרעה . . .
Now you shall see what I will do to Pharaoh . . .

A person lying on his deathbed will experience a brief resurgence of life; he will sit up and may even request some nourishment. It is a natural phenomenon that the more a person senses his imminent and inevitable demise, the more he will resist it.

The words "now you shall see," which Hashem addressed to Moshe, were predicated on this phenomenon. The very fact that Pharaoh persisted ever more strongly in wickedness provides the clearest evidence of his impending downfall.

Kli Yakar

Vo'aira / וארא

וידעתם כי אני ה' אלקיכם ... והבאתי אתכם אל הארץ
And you shall know that I am Hashem your Lord ... And I will bring you to the land

It is difficult to understand that on the one hand Hashem promised entry into the holy land to the generation that came out of Egypt, yet that entire generation perished during the forty years of wandering in the desert. A closer look at the text reveals the answer.

The redemption and exodus from Egypt were heralded with the following four expressions of freedom (*Shemos* 6:6-7): *vehotzaisi* (and I will bring out), *vehitzalti* (and I will deliver), *vega'alti* (and I will redeem) and *velakachti* (and I will take).

The fifth expression, *vehavaisi* (and I will bring you) is the promise of entry into the land. This expression, however, does not follow immediately after the four expressions of freedom, being interrupted by the expression *veyadatem* (and you shall know that I am Hashem your Lord) in the abovementioned verse. It is as if to say that the coming into the

[ו:ז-ח] ולקחתי אתכם לי לעם והייתי לכם לאלקים וידעתם כי אני ה' אלקיכם המוציא אתכם מתחת סבלות מצרים. והבאתי אתכם אל הארץ אשר נשאתי את ידי לתת אתה לאברהם ליצחק וליעקב ונתתי אתה לכם מורשה אני ה'.

[6:7-8] "And I will take you to Me for a people, and I will be a Lord to you; and you shall know that I am Hashem your Lord, who brings you out from under the burdens of the Egyptians. And I will bring you to the land which I swore with My upraised Hand to give to Avraham, to Yitzchak, and to Yaakov, and I will give it to you for a heritage; I am Hashem."

TORAH TREASURES • *Vo'aira*

land is contingent on *veyadatem*. Without this knowledge of Hashem, you will merit only the redemption but not entry to the land.

And thus, when they sinned, they forfeited the promise of "I will bring you to the land," for without *veyadatem* there is no *vehavaisi*.

Or Hachayim

[ט: ו] וידבר משה כן אל בני ישראל ולא שמעו אל משה מקצר רוח ומעבדה קשה.

[6:9] **And Moshe spoke so to the people of Yisrael, but they did not listen to Moshe because of their dispiritedness and hard labors.**

... ולא שמעו אל משה
... but they did not listen to Moshe

Based on various *Midrashic* interpretations of the name Moshe, an original homiletic exposition of the abovementioned verse emerges.

It is written (*Shemos* 2:10): "And the child grew, and she brought him to Pharaoh's daughter, and he became her son, and she named him Moshe, and she said: 'Because I drew him out of the water.'" The question arises: If this were the reason for his name, why didn't she name him Mashooy, which means the one who was drawn, in the passive form, rather than Moshe, which means the one who draws, in the active form? Several answers can be suggested.

By naming him Moshe (in the active form), Pharaoh's daughter wished to indicate that he would "draw her out" of the fires of Gehinnom. She already had renounced her father's idol worship and had beheld the Divine Presence which surrounded the infant Moshe. According to the *Zohar*, she also had converted to the faith of Yisrael and for her humane act of rescuing Moshe she merited entering into Gan Eden. All this is implied in the verse: "He became her son, and she named him Moshe." He became her son by virtue of her rescue, thus she called him Moshe, for he was to

וארא • TORAH TREASURES

deliver her from perdition.

One might ask, how could she publicly repudiate her father's beliefs by naming him Moshe, "the one who delivers me from Gehinnom," while her evil father occupied the mighty throne of Egypt?

In order to quell any suspicion of heresy she explained the meaning of the name Moshe "because I drew him out of the water," thus concealing its true meaning.

The text itself corroborates this interpretation. If the Torah would have stated that she called him Moshe "because I drew him out of the water," the implication would then have been that this was her true motive for calling him Moshe. The text differs in one important nuance. It reads: "She named him Moshe, and she said: 'Because I drew him out of the water.'" By adding these words the Torah subtly wants to tell us that the true reason for the name Moshe was "that he would save her from Gehinnom," whereas the ostensible reason was "because I drew him out of the water."

Alternatively, it can be suggested that Hashem implanted in her mind the thought of naming him Moshe for her own reasons, but Hashem's reason for wanting him to be named Moshe was because he would lead the Jewish people out of bondage.

A third reason can be found in the numerical value of the name משה, *Moshe*, which equals that of א-ל ש-ד-י, *the Almighty Lord*. The underlying meaning of this *gematria* is that Moshe would lead Yisrael to freedom in the merit of the *Avos* to Whom Hashem appeared with the Name of א-ל ש-ד-י, which is the Divine Attribute of bringing an end to affliction. Thus, א-ל ש-ד-י will show mercy and through Moshe will bring an end to their afflic-

[ו:ט] וידבר משה כן אל
בני ישראל ולא שמעו אל
משה מקצר רוח ומעבדה
קשה.

[6:9] And Moshe spoke so to the people of Yisrael, but they did not listen to Moshe because of their dispiritedness and hard labors.

tion (compare Rashi in *Beraishis* 43:14).

The verse "and they did not to listen Moshe" can now be interpreted to mean that they did not understand the reasons or the *gematria* behind the name Moshe, which implied that he would lead them to freedom.

Chomas Anoch

[ז:ט] כי ידבר אלכם פרעה לאמר תנו לכם מופת ואמרת אל אהרן קח את מטך והשלך לפני פרעה יהי לתנין.

[7:9] "When Pharaoh shall speak to you, saying: 'Show a sign for yourselves,' then you shall say to Aharon: 'Take your staff and cast it down before Pharaoh that it may become a serpent.'"

תנו לכם מופת . . .

Show a sign for yourselves . . .

We would expect the text to state, "Show a sign for us."

When a sorcerer casts a spell or performs a magic act he astounds and enraptures his spectators. The sorcerer himself is not impressed, for he knows that his performance is based on illusion, deception, and sleight of hand.

By contrast, when Hashem performs a miracle through His prophet, the prophet is only Hashem's messenger and he himself marvels at this manifestation of Divine Power. This is implied by the phrase: "Show a sign for yourselves." Show me a true miracle, one which shall be a wondrous sign for you too.

Rabbi Elimelech of Lizhensk

[ח:ב] ויט אהרן את ידו על מימי מצרים ותעל הצפרדע ותכס את ארץ מצרים.

[8:2] And Aharon stretched out his hand over the waters of Egypt, and the frogs came up and covered the land of Egypt.

ותעל הצפרדע . . .

And the frogs came up . . .

The precise reading is "and the frog came up," in the singular. Rashi explains that there was originally only one frog, but when the Egyptians struck it, it split into myriad frogs.

When the Egyptians observed that striking the frogs caused them to multiply immeasurably, common sense would dictate that they stop striking them. But a person who acts in

וארא • TORAH TREASURES

anger does not listen to the voice of reason. The more the Egyptians struck the frogs, the faster they multiplied, until "they covered the land of Egypt."

This cycle of anger begetting more anger occurred not only in Egypt; it is characteristic of all quarrels, whenever and wherever they may erupt.

In any dispute, as in Egypt, if the aggrieved party would remain silent, then the squabble would gradually subside. Regrettably, the opposite is true. Accusations and recriminations are voiced, provoking a torrent of counter claims, acrimony and name calling. Ultimately, the bickering escalates into a crescendo of uncontrollable rage, a perfect parallel to the plague of the frogs.

Birkas Peretz

... ויצעק משה אל ה' על דבר הצפרדעים אשר שם לפרעה
...**and Moshe cried out to Hashem concerning the frogs which He had brought on Pharaoh**

The specific reiteration of the purpose for the frogs as part of Moshe's prayer seems superfluous in the context of the verse. The inclusion of this phrase, however, teaches us a fundamental lesson with regard to prayer. When praying one should not say, "Since Hashem knows my needs and the anguish that is in my heart, a general prayer for health and well-being will suffice." Just as Moshe spelled out his prayer in detail, so must we define and articulate our prayerful requests specifically.

Or Hachayim

[ח:ח] ויצא משה ואהרן מעם פרעה ויצעק משה אל ה' על דבר הצפרדעים אשר שם לפרעה.

[8:8] **And Moshe and Aharon left the presence of Pharaoh, and Moshe cried out to Hashem concerning the frogs which He had brought on Pharaoh.**

Bo / בא

... לראת את הארץ
... to see the earth

This entire verse refers to the locusts, except for the phrase "that one will not be able to see the earth," which refers to the people.

Some commentaries, however, suggest that this phrase also refers to the locusts. Recalling the rabbinic maxim that the blind are never satiated by the food they eat, this phrase serves as an explanation for the total destruction wrought by locust swarms. Since there were so many locusts that they were unable to see the land, they developed insatiable appetites.

Chomas Anoch

[י:ה] וכסה את עין הארץ ולא יוכל לראת את הארץ ואכל את יתר הפלטה הנשארת לכם מן הברד ואכל את כל העץ הצמח לכם מן השדה.

[10:5] "And they will cover the face of the earth, that one will not be able to see the earth, and they will eat the remainder of residue of that which is left from the hailstorm, and they will eat all your trees that grow in the field."

... ואנחנו לא נדע מה נעבד את ה' עד באנו שמה
... and we will not know with what to serve Hashem, until we come there

The Rebbe of Gur interprets this verse in a metaphorical style, thereby expressing a profound thought.

[י:כו] וגם מקננו ילך עמנו לא תשאר פרסה כי ממנו נקח לעבד את ה' אלקינו ואנחנו לא נדע מה נעבד את ה' עד באנו שמה.

[10:26] "Our cattle

also shall go with us, there shall not be a hoof left behind, for we must take from it to serve Hashem our Lord, and we will not know with what to serve Hashem, until we come there."

[יא:ז] ולכל בני ישראל לא יחרץ כלב לשנו למאיש ועד בהמה למען תדעון אשר יפלה ה' בין מצרים ובין ישראל.

[11:7] But no dog shall whet his tongue against any of the people of Yisrael, against man or animal, so that you may know that Hashem has differentiated between Egypt and Yisrael.

He states that we cannot gauge the true value of our service to Hashem until we reach "there," the higher world, the World to Come. Only then will we learn whether our divine worship was pleasing to Hashem.

Rabbi Yitzchak Meir of Gur

ולכל בני ישראל לא יחרץ כלב לשנו . . .
But no dog shall whet his tongue against any of the people of Yisrael . . .

A tale is told of a man who came to Rabbi Meir of Premyshlan for advice.

"I have devised all manner of clever schemes and maneuvers in order to become successful in business," he complained, "but the more I try the more I fail."

"You can find the answer to your problem," replied Rabbi Meir, "in the verse ולכל בני ישראל לא יחרץ כלב לשנו , *but no dog shall whet his tongue against any of the people of Yisrael.* יחרץ, *to whet or sharpen,* can also mean *to be cunning or sly.* כלב, *a dog,* can also be read as *kilaiv,* like a heart. In this sense, the verse will read that all the people of Yisrael will not have to resort to cunning or slyness, so long as their tongues speak what is in their hearts. Be frank and straightforward in business. Forget about schemes and trickery, and I promise you success in all your endeavors."

Al Hatorah

[יב:ב] החדש הזה לכם ראש חדשים ראשון הוא לכם לחדשי השנה.

[12:2] This month shall be the beginning of months for you, it shall be the

החדש הזה . . .
This month . . .

The month in which Yisrael's redemption occurred is called ניסן, *Nissan,* which is a derivation of the word נס, *miracle,* a reminder of the many miracles that took place during this

בא • TORAH TREASURES

month. A closer investigation of the word נס yields a wealth of concepts that far transcends its English equivalent of miracle.

The word נס is composed of the letters נ, *nun*, and ס, *samach*.

The letter *nun* is especially significant. It is well known that for the initial letters of the verses of *Ashrei* (*Tehillim* 145) David Hamelech followed the order of the *aleph bais*. Yet, there is no verse beginning with the initial letter *nun*. Our Sages tell us that this is because the initial letter נ contains an allusion to Yisrael's period of נפילה, *downfall*, recalling the verse, נפלה לא תוסיף קום בתולת ישראל, "*The virgin of Yisrael is fallen, she shall rise no more.*" (*Amos* 5:2) Nevertheless, knowing that the downfall would take place, David Hamelech comforts Yisrael by saying in the verse beginning with the letter ס, *samach*: סומך ה' לכל הנופלים, "*Hashem supports all the fallen ones.*"

Thus we note that *nun* symbolizes downfall and *samach* symbolizes support or aid. The word נס, incorporating both these letters, inspires within us the hope for a miraculous deliverance that will follow on the heels of the darkest night of oppression and adversity.

Bnei Yisaschar

החדש הזה לכם ראש חדשים . . .
This month shall be the beginning of months for you . . .

One segment in the liturgy of the Blessing of the New Moon is the recitation of *Mi She'asah Nissim:* "He Who performed miracles for our forefathers and redeemed them from slavery to freedom, may He redeem us soon. . ."

The *mitzvah* of *Rosh Chodesh*, as indicated

first month of the year for you.

[יב:ב] החדש הזה לכם ראש חדשים ראשון הוא לכם לחדשי השנה.

[12:2] This month shall be the beginning of months for you, it shall be the first month of the year for you.

145

in the above verse, was an integral part of the process of redemption and delivery. With our *Rosh Chodesh* prayer we ask Hashem for a continuation of this miraculous salvation in our days, to culminate with "the ingathering of our dispersed from the four corners of the earth." We state, in effect, that just as He redeemed our forefathers in the merit of the *mitzvah* of *Rosh Chodesh*, so may we be worthy of His deliverance today in the merit of our observance of this same *mitzvah*.

Tosefes Berachah

[יב:ד] ואם ימעט הבית מהיות משה ולקח הוא ושכנו הקרב אל ביתו במכסת נפשת איש לפי אכלו תכסו על השה.

[12:4] **And if the household be too small for a lamb, then he and his neighbor whose house is nearby take one according to the number of souls, according to every man's eating shall you make your count for the lamb.**

איש לפי אכלו ...
according to every man's eating ...

The numerical value of איש לפי אכלו, *according to every man's eating*, is equivalent to that of אכל כזית, *one must eat a measure equivalent to an olive.* This *gematria* is a reflection of the *Halachah* which states that anyone eating less than the quantity of an olive of the *Pesach* sacrifice has not fulfilled his obligation.

Mahara of Worms

[יב:יד] והיה היום הזה לכם לזכרון וחגתם אתו חג לה' לדרתיכם חקת עולם תחגהו.

[12:14] **And this day shall be a memorial for you, and you shall celebrate it as a festival to Hashem, you shall celebrate it as an everlasting law for all your generations.**

... וחגתם אותו חג לה' לדרתיכם חקת עולם תחגהו
... and you shall celebrate it as a festival to Hashem, you shall celebrate it as an everlasting law for all your generations

The words "a festival to Hashem" underscore the true meaning of *Pesach.*

A person living in modern times who views *Yetzias Mitzraim*, the Exodus from Egypt, merely as an ancient tribe's attainment of freedom from physical bondage may justifiably wonder why it is important to celebrate an event from the distant past. On the other hand, if he understands that the Exodus represents a spiritual transformation of an entire nation from a state of impurity to sanctity, from the mundane to the timeless, then he will truly rejoice, regardless of the times or circumstances under which he lives.

This is what the verse is telling us. If we celebrate it as a festival to Hashem, in its spiritual sense, then we will celebrate it as an everlasting law for all our generations.

Meshech Chochmah

[יב:יח] בראשן בארבעה עשר יום לחדש בערב תאכלו מצת עד יום האחד ועשרים לחדש בערב.

[12:18] In the first month, on the fourteenth day of the month in the evening, you shall eat unleavened bread, until the twenty first day of the month in the evening.

... בערב תאכלו מצת
... in the evening, you shall eat unleavened bread

The word מצת, *unleavened bread*, in this verse is written in the abbreviated form, without a ו, *vav*. Some commentaries suggest this is because this shorter form constitutes the acronym of the words צדקה תציל ממות, *the giving of charity protects one from death*.

This close link between the *mitzvos* of *matzoh* and giving charity finds expression in the universal custom of giving *ma'os chittim*, money given to the needy for matzos and *Pesach* food.

Otzar Chaim

[יב:כג] ועבר ה' לנגף את מצרים וראה את הדם על המשקוף ועל שתי המזוזת ופסח ה' על הפתח ולא יתן המשחית לבא אל בתיכם לנגף.

[12:23] And Hashem will pass through to strike the Egyptians, and when He sees the blood upon the lintel and on the two sideposts, Hashem will

... ולא יתן המשחית לבא אל בתיכם לנגף
... and will not allow the destroyer to come into your houses to strike you

This verse appears to be inconsistent with the well-known statement in the *Haggadah* that the plague of the slaying of the firstborn was executed by Hashem Himself, as it is written: "For I will go through the land of Egypt," (*Shemos* 12:12) I and not an angel, I and not a Seraph... By contrast, the abovementioned verse indicates that a destroyer and not

Hashem struck down the Egyptians. The Vilna Gaon reconciles these conflicting statements.

The plague of the slaying of the firstborn was most certainly carried out by Hashem. However, as was to be expected, that night as at all other times there were Jews who were near death from natural causes simply because the time of their demise had arrived. The *malach hamavess*, the angel of death, could be reasonably expected at these homes.

Our verse tells us that during that night Hashem would not permit the destroyer, the angel of death, to enter even these houses so as not to offer the Egyptians a pretext for ascribing the death of their firstborn to natural phenomena, pointing out the Jews who had also died that night.

Vilna Gaon

והיה כי יאמרו אליכם בניכם מה העבדה הזאת לכם ואמרתם זבח פסח הוא לה'...

And it shall come to pass, when your children will say to you: "What does this service mean to you?" Then you shall say: "It is the Passover sacrifice for Hashem . . ."

In the *Haggadah*, the wicked son asks the question mentioned in this verse, "What does this service mean to you?"

His wickedness is evident in the way he phrases the question, "to you" but not to me, thereby excluding himself from the Jewish people.

The response he receives is the quotation: "It is because of what Hashem did for me when he rescued me from Egypt." (*Shemos* 13:8) The emphasis is on "me." Hashem did it for me, but not for him; had he been there, he would not have been redeemed.

בא • TORAH TREASURES

The response the *Haggadah* offers is taken from *Shemos* 13:8. The Torah, however, gives a different answer to this question in the abovementioned verse: "It is the Passover sacrifice for Hashem..." Why does the *Haggadah* overlook the response specifically addressed to this question and uses instead an apparently unrelated quotation in the next chapter that appears unrelated to this question?

It seems the *Haggadah* did not consider this verse, "It is the Passover sacrifice..." to be the fitting answer to the wicked son. Inasmuch as he denies the basic tenets of the Jewish faith and contemptuously excludes himself from the ranks of the Jewish people, it is futile to enter into philosophical disputations with him. He has to be silenced with a crushing retort, as that in verse 13:8.

A closer analysis of the abovementioned verse reveals an insight in support of this thesis. The Torah states, "You shall say." Not "You shall say to him," nor "You shall say to your son." This is a clear indication that the subsequent statement is not intended as a reply to the wicked son. Rather, it is designed to inspire and buttress those who hear the wicked son's question, that they not be disheartened by his scornful attitude towards the *mitzvos*.

Vilna Gaon

ואמרתם זבח פסח הוא לה'...
Then you shall say: "It is the Passover sacrifice for Hashem..."

A *Midrash Peliah*, a perplexing *Midrash*, finds a clue in this verse to the rule that thirty days before a festival arrives we begin to discuss and make inquiries into the laws of that festival.

our houses"; and the people bowed and prostrated themselves.

[יב:כז] ואמרתם זבח פסח הוא לה' אשר פסח על בתי בני ישראל במצרים בנגפו את מצרים ואת בתינו הציל ויקד העם וישתחוו.

[12:27] Then you shall say: "It is the Passover sacrifice

TORAH TREASURES • Bo

for Hashem, that He passed over the houses of the people of Yisrael in Egypt when He struck the Egyptians, sparing our houses;" and the people bowed and prostrated themselves.

[יב:מב] ליל שמרים הוא לה' להוציאם מארץ מצרים הוא הלילה הזה לה' שמרים לכל בני ישראל לדרתם.

[12:42] It was a vigil night for Hashem, for bringing them out from the land of Egypt; this same night is a vigil night for Hashem for all the people of Yisrael for all their generations.

[יג:טז] והיה לאות על ידכה ולטוטפת בין עיניך כי בחזק יד הוציאנו ה' ממצרים.

[13:16] And it shall be a sign upon your hand and for a remembrance between your eyes, that the law of Hashem may be in your mouth, for Hashem has brought you out of Egypt with a strong Hand.

A possible correlation between the verse and this rule emerges when the words זבח פסח, *the Passover sacrifice*, are read with a slight variation in the vowelization whereby they can be read as "cut the word Pesach in half." Thus, half of פ, 80, becomes מ, 40, half of ס, 60, becomes ל, 30, and half of ח, 8, becomes ד, 4.

The resulting letters *mem, lamed* and *daled*, form the word למד, *lamed*, which has two meanings. It denotes the letter *lamed*, which has a numerical value of 30, and it is also a verb meaning to learn or study. Thus, thirty days before the festival we must begin to study in preparation for it.

Iturei Torah

... ליל שמרים הוא לה' להוציאם
It was a vigil night for Hashem, for bringing them out ...

The initial letters of הוא לה' להוציאם, *it was for Hashem, for bringing them out*, combine to form the word הלל, *Hallel*, alluding to the fact that *Hallel* is recited on the night of *Pesach*.

Mahara of Worms

... ולטוטפת בין עיניך
...and for a remembrance between your eyes

The numerical value of these words ולטוטפת בין עיניך equals that of אלו ארבע בתים, *they consist of four compartments*. This *gematria* is indicative of the precept that only the תפילין של יד, *the arm tefillin*, are made as one undivided capsule, while the תפילין של ראש, *the head tefillin*, have four separate compartments.

Chomas Anoch

Beshalach / בשלח

ויקח משה את עצמות יוסף עמו . . .
And Moshe took the bones of Yosef with him . . .

The *Midrash* expounds the verse (*Mishlei* 10:8), "The wise in heart will take *mitzvos*" as referring to Moshe, who was occupied taking the bones of Yosef with him while all Israel was busy gathering the spoils of Egypt.

The question arises: Didn't gathering the spoils of Egypt also constitute the fulfillment of a *mitzvah*? Indeed, Hashem had said to Moshe (*ibid.* 11:2): "Speak now in the ears of the people and let each of them ask of his friend, and each woman of her friend, objects of silver and objects of gold". Weren't the people of Yisrael complying with this command when they busied themselves with gathering the spoils of Egypt? Why then does the *Midrash* single out Moshe, praising him for the performance of his *mitzvah*?

Comparing the two *mitzvos* we find that being occupied with Yosef's bones deprived Moshe of the monetary gain that would have accrued to him had he instead gathered the

[יג:יט] ויקח משה את עצמות יוסף עמו כי השבע השביע את בני ישראל לאמר פקד יפקד אלקים אתכם והעליתם את עצמתי מזה אתכם.

[13:19] And Moshe took the bones of Yosef with him, for he had bound the people of Yisrael by oath, saying: "The Lord will surely remember you, and then you shall carry up my bones with you from here."

151

spoils of Egypt. Consequently, the lesson to be derived from the *Midrash* is that a person who performs a *mitzvah* which involves financial loss is deemed more virtuous and commendable than one who performs a *mitzvah* which, by its very nature, results in a handsome profit.

Al Hatorah

[יד: ה] ויגד למלך מצרים כי ברח העם ויהפך לבב פרעה ועבדיו אל העם ויאמרו מה זאת עשינו כי שלחנו את ישראל מעבדנו.

[14:5] **And it was told to the king of Egypt that the people had fled, and the feelings of Pharaoh and his servants about the people changed, and they said: "What is this we have done that we have released Yisrael from serving us?"**

ויגד למלך מצרים כי ברח העם...
And it was told to the king of Egypt that the people had fled...

The text uses the impersonal verb form ויגד, *and it was told*, but it does not specify who told the king. However, Rabbeinu Efraim points out that, by means of a *gematria*, the Torah alludes to his true identity.

The numerical value of כי ברח, *that (the people) had fled*, equals that of עמלק, *Amalek*. Thus, Amalek is identified as the one who reported כי ברח, *"that (the people) had fled."*

Likewise, it was Amalek who reported to Lavan that Yaakov had fled. We find in this connection an analogous text (*Beraishis* 31:22): ויגד ללבן ביום השלישי כי ברח יעקב, *"And it was told to Lavan on the third day that Yaakov had fled."* In this case also, the equation of עמלק = כי ברח applies, telling us that Amalek was the informer.

Chomas Anoch

Author's note:

The *Midrash*, indeed, explicitly states that Amalek informed Lavan of Yaakov's flight and similarly reported to Pharaoh the escape of the people of Yisrael.

בשלח • TORAH TREASURES

ויגד למלך מצרים כי ברח העם ...
And it was told to the king of Egypt that the people had fled...

Our Sages teach us that the men of the tribe of Efraim escaped from Egypt thirty years prior to *Yetzias Mitzraim*, the Exodus from Egypt, but that they were subsequently killed by the Philistines.

We may assume that Pharaoh's magicians advised him that Yisrael's most recent attempt at gaining freedom after 210 years of bondage would be equally abortive, like the escape of the men of Efraim. Indeed, any exodus prior to the end of the 400 years of divinely ordained enslavement seemed doomed. Thus, Pharaoh's advisors counseled, the people of Yisrael would never reach the Promised Land. Instead, they would be led into captivity by the Babylonians or another mighty nation in that region. A *gematria* found in this verse serves to confirm that this was their line of reasoning.

Focusing on כי ברח we note that the numerical value of כי equals 30, alluding to the escape of the men of Efraim 30 years before *Yetzias Mitzraim*. The numerical value of ברח equals 210, hinting at the 210 years of slavery that had elapsed at the time of the Exodus. The juxtaposition of כי and ברח signifies the fact that they are comparable in that both events occurred prior to the end of the predestined 400 years of slavery and that they were therefore both doomed to failure.

Pharaoh's reaction was ויהפך לבב פרעה, *and Pharaoh had a change of heart*, ויאמרו מה זאת עשינו כי שלחנו את ישראל מעבדנו, *and they said: "What is this we have done that we have released Yisrael from serving us?"*

The word לבב, *heart*, is composed of the same letters as the word בבל, *Babylonia*.

[יד:ה] ויגד למלך מצרים כי ברח העם ויהפך לבב פרעה ועבדיו אל העם ויאמרו מה זאת עשינו כי שלחנו את ישראל מעבדנו.

[14:5] And it was told to the king of Egypt that the people had fled, and the feelings of Pharaoh and his servants about the people changed, and they said: "What is this we have done that we have released Yisrael from serving us?"

TORAH TREASURES • *Beshalach*

Thus, Pharaoh's change of heart was prompted by his realization that Yisrael would now be enslaved by Babylonia, rather than remain under the domination of Egypt.

Consequently, his anger was aroused not only by the loss of his Jewish slaves, but also by the fact that someone else, Babylonia in this case, would now gain the services of "his" runaway slaves.

Chomas Anoch

[יד:יג] ויאמר משה אל העם אל תיראו התיצבו וראו את ישועת ה' אשר יעשה לכם היום כי אשר ראיתם את מצרים היום לא תספו לראתם עוד עד עולם.

[14:13] **And Moshe said to the people: "Do not fear. Stand still and see the salvation of Hashem, which He will work for you today, for although you see the Egyptians today, you shall see them no more forever."**

... התיצבו וראו את ישועת ה'...
Stand still and see the salvation of Hashem ...

These epic words were uttered by Moshe, heralding the great miracle of *Kriyas Yam Suf*, the parting of the Sea of Reeds.

The numerical value of התיצבו, *stand still*, is equal to that of חתן, *groom,* and כלה, *bride.* This *gematria* recalls the well-known rabbinic aphorism: "Finding a suitable match is as difficult as the parting of the Sea of Reeds."

An alternate interpretation suggests that the *gematria* meant to hold out the promise that the people of Yisrael were to be saved in the merit of the Stand at Mount Sinai, at which time Israel would be given in marriage, so to speak, to Hashem.

Chomas Anoch

... כי אשר ראיתם את מצרים היום לא תספו לראתם עוד עד עולם
... for although you see the Egyptians today, you shall see them no more forever

This verse served as the basis for a *Halachic* decision rendered by Rabbi Yechezkel Landau, author of *Noda Biyehudah*. This is the background of the case.

Two brothers who were partners in business lived for many years in peace and harmony. Quite unexpectedly, a disagreement arose between them, and before long, their amicable relationship was replaced by quarreling and bitter hatred. The altercation reached a point that one brother, fuming with rage, took a solemn oath never to see his brother again. The other brother, learning of the vow, became so depressed that it affected his health, and he died soon after that.

The surviving brother, now filled with remorse, wanted to beg his dead brother's forgiveness, but his solemn vow, still being in force, deterred him. He inquired of the rabbis of his city and they agreed unanimously that his vow was subject to annulment. They based their ruling on the *Talmudic* supposition that "this was not the intent of his oath"; in other words, when he took the oath, presumably he did not have the intent to be prohibited from seeing his dead brother's face.

When the case was brought before Rabbi Yechezkel Landau, who at the time was still a very young man, he replied that this vow required no annulment. He based his ruling on the abovementioned verse. This divine promise, he argued, surely carries as much weight as a personal vow. Yet, in verse 14:30 we read: "And Yisrael saw the Egyptians dead upon the seashore," indicating that they did see them again. Clearly, seeing a person after his death is not considered "seeing" him.

An objection was raised to this ruling on the grounds that verse 14:30 does not prove that the people of Yisrael saw the Egyptians close-up; perhaps they saw their bodies only from a distance. Rabbi Yechezkel Landau refuted this argument by citing the *Midrash* which states

[יד:יג] ויאמר משה אל העם אל תיראו התיצבו וראו את ישועת ה' אשר יעשה לכם היום כי אשר ראיתם את מצרים היום לא תספו לראתם עוד עד עולם.

[14:13] And Moshe said to the people: "Do not fear. Stand still and see the salvation of Hashem, which He will work for you today, for although you see the Egyptians today, you shall see them no more forever."

TORAH TREASURES • *Beshalach*

that every Jew recognized among the dead Egyptians the face of his task-master and tormentor, which could only be accomplished from close proximity.

Iturei Torah

Author's note:
It is noteworthy that the *Mechilta* expounds the verse (14:31): "And Yisrael saw the Egyptians dead upon the seashore," to mean that they were "dead but not quite dead," in other words that they were dying. Similarly, in the *piyut* (liturgical poem) of the last day of *Pesach* we read: "You stretched out your right hand, they were dead, yet not quite dead; their spirit was still within their body."

According to this, there is no proof from the verses as to whether "seeing" one who is dead requires an annulment. The contradictory verses (14:14 and 14:30), may possibly be reconciled by rendering "today" in verse 14:14 literally, meaning the entire day. And indeed, when the people of Yisrael saw the dead bodies of the Egyptians washed up on the seashore it was still the same day.

[יד:יד] ה' ילחם לכם ואתם תחרשון.

[14:14] "Hashem will fight for you, and you shall remain silent."

ה' ילחם לכם ואתם תחרשון
Hashem will fight for you, and you shall remain silent

The *Mechilta* expounds this verse stating, "Not only will He fight for you at that time, but for all eternity will He battle for you against your enemies."

For a better understanding of this *Midrash* we must recognize that at the time of *Yetzias Mitzraim*, when the people of Yisrael found themselves pursued by the mighty Egyptian army, they confronted Hashem with a compelling argument: "Why did you bring us forth out of Egypt?" Out of necessity, Hashem was obliged then to fight for them.

At that time, Hashem also assured the people of Yisrael that He would always do battle for them, even when they would have no rightful claim to His help. Indeed, there would come a time when Yisrael will only be able to say, "Ours is the shamefacedness," (Daniel 9:7) but even then will He fight for them.

Our verse can be interpreted to express this thought. "Hashem will fight for you" even when "you remain silent," meaning, even when you have no convincing claim to Hashem's help, He will nonetheless defend you against your adversaries.

Meshech Chochmah

מה תצעק אלי דבר . . .
Why do you cry out to me? Speak . . .

The final letters of the words מה תצעק אלי דבר, *Why do you cry out to me? Speak*, form the word הקיר, *the wall*. This is an allusion to the precept that when praying one should stand directly in front of a wall.

This concept is mentioned explicitly in connection with King Chizkiah: "Then he turned his face to the wall and prayed." (*Melachim* II 20:2)

Rabbeinu Efraim

[יד:טו] ויאמר ה' אל משה מה תצעק אלי דבר אל בני ישראל ויסעו.

[14:15] And Hashem said to Moshe: "Why do you cry out to me? Speak to the people of Yisrael that they go forward."

ויט משה את ידו על הים . . . ויבקעו המים
And Moshe stretched out his hand over the sea . . . and the waters were divided

The *Midrash* expounds the verse: "The sea saw and fled." (*Tehillim* 114:3) What did it see? It saw the *Beraisa* of Rabbi Yishmael.

What is the meaning of this *Midrash*?

[יד:כא] ויט משה את ידו על הים ויולך ה' את הים ברוח קדים עזה כל הלילה וישם את הים לחרבה ויבקעו המים.

[14:21] And Moshe stretched out his hand over the sea,

TORAH TREASURES • *Beshalach*

and Hashem caused the sea to go back by a strong east wind all the night, and He made the sea into dry land, and the waters were divided.

Initially, we note an apparent inconsistency in the syntax of the *Tehillim* verse itself. הים ראה וינס, *The sea saw and fled.* הירדן יסב לאחור, *The Jordan (River) will turn back.* "The first phrase uses the past tense, the latter the future tense. We would expect the second segment to read הירדן נסב לאחור, *the Jordan turned back*, also in the past tense.

The contrast in tenses can be explained if we translate the verse as follows: "The sea saw and fled," because "the Jordan will turn back." In other words, the sea saw that at a future time the Jordan River would part its waters to allow Yehoshua to pass through upon entering Eretz Israel. (*Yehoshua* 4:16-17) Seeing this, the sea applied the rule of *kal vachomer* (a *fortiriori* reasoning), saying, "If the Jordan parts its waters before a disciple of Moshe, then I must certainly part my waters before Moshe himself."

Now, the "incomprehensible" *Midrash* becomes clear. What did the sea see? It saw the *Beraisa* of Rabbi Yishmael in which he enumerated the thirteen rules by which the Torah is expounded, one of which is the *kal vachomer*, the logical inference. The sea saw and made use of this rule, "and the waters were divided."

Kehillas Yitzchak

[טו:א] אז ישיר משה ובני ישראל את השירה הזאת לה' ויאמרו לאמר אשירה לה' כי גאה גאה סוס ורכבו רמה בים.

[15:1] **Moshe and the people of Yisrael then sang this song**

אז ישיר משה ובני ישראל . . .
Moshe and the people of Yisrael then sang . . .

The *Midrash* comments: "Moshe said, I sinned by using the word אז, *then*, for I said, ומאז באתי אל פרעה לדבר בשמך הרע לעם הזה, *From the time I came to Pharaoh to speak in Your name he has dealt ill with this people.*

(5:23) Now I shall begin my song of praise with the same word אז."

One may wonder how the use of אז in the *Shirah* can make amends for the prior use of אז in an improper context.

Let us consider an individual whom Hashem delivered from anguish and sorrow, who now offers praises and gratitude to Hashem. He expresses gladness for his rescue, but he certainly does not rejoice in the pain and trouble from which he was saved.

By contrast, when Moshe and the people of Yisrael proclaimed the glorious *Shirah*, the Song of the Sea, they were inspired not only by the miraculous events they had witnessed but also by their being the instrument of revelation of Hashem's glory. For through their salvation Hashem's greatness became known throughout the world. Thus, the *Shirah* was a hymn both in praise of the redemption and in expressing their salvation from bondage, for without bondage there can be no redemption.

This then is what Moshe said: "I confess that I sinned when I used the word אז, for in the verse beginning with אז I complained about the unbearable severity of our servitude. But now I raise my voice in a song of praise, commencing with אז, a song inspired by our redemption as well as our suffering."

Thus, the protest against suffering is atoned for by a song of praise inspired by suffering.

Similarly, David Hamelech states: "I thank You, for You have afflicted me and become my salvation." (*Tehillim* 118:21) I offer thanks to You for the pain You inflicted on me, for the pain was the source of my salvation, and through me Your Name was glorified.

Bais Halevi

to Hashem, and they said, saying: "I will sing to Hashem for He is highly exalted; He has hurled the horse and its rider into the sea."

TORAH TREASURES • *Beshalach*

[טו:ב] עזי וזמרת קה ויהי לי לישועה זה קלי ואנוהו אלקי אבי וארממנהו.

[15:2] "Hashem is my strength and song, and He became my salvation; this is my Lord, and I will glorify Him, the Lord of my father, and I will exalt Him."

זה קלי ואנוהו ...

This is my Lord, and I will glorify Him ...

To remake oneself in Hashem's image constitutes Hashem's glorification. One's virtuous deeds and devout posture are a reflection of Hashem's splendor in the world.

Maharal

... זה קלי ואנוהו אלקי אבי וארממנהו

... This is my Lord, and I will glorify Him, the Lord of my father, and I will exalt Him

Rashi, quoting *Mechilta*, comments that at the parting of the sea a common maidservant beheld a greater manifestation of Hashem's Presence than all the prophets saw in their heavenly prophecies.

How is this vision by a maidservant reflected in this verse?

The connection may be established by examining the *Mishnah* (*Bikkurim* 1:4): "A *ger*, proselyte, offers the *bikkurim*, first fruits, but does not recite the *bikkurim* declaration (*Devarim* 26:3), because it contains the phrase, 'I have come to the land which Hashem swore to our fathers,' which is not applicable to a *ger*."

Now, in the abovementioned verse we find two phrases.

"This is my Lord...the Lord of my father..." They perceived Hashem as their personal Lord and as their ancestral Lord. The *Mechilta* sees in this dual perception a hint for its statement regarding the maidservant.

"This is my Lord" was said by those who were unable to say "the Lord of my father," namely the non-Jews who had joined in the

Exodus, among whom were included the maidservant. "The Lord of my father" was said by the people of Yisrael.

Vilna Gaon

... נשפת ברוחך כסמו ים
You blew with Your wind, the sea covered them ...

The combination of the last letters of the four words נשפת ברוחך כסמו ים, *You blew with Your wind, the sea covered them*, yields the term מכות, *plagues*.

This indicates that at the Sea of Reeds, in addition to being drowned, the Egyptians suffered a great number of other afflictions, as stated in the *Haggadah*.

The Sage who states in the *Haggadah* that at the sea they suffered fifty plagues can find additional support for his contention in the word ים, *sea*, whose numerical value equals 50.

Nachal Kedumim

... כי מרים הם
... for they were bitter

One might suggest that the phrase "for they were bitter" does not refer to the waters at all. Rather, it expresses the acrimony that possessed Yisrael's spirit. The repulsive taste of the water was attributed to their resentful mood. Indeed, to an angry person even the sweetest delicacy will leave a bitter aftertaste. The waters were sweet, but "they could not drink them, for they (the people of Yisrael) were bitter."

Daas Chachamim

[טו:י] נשפת ברוחך כסמו ים צללו כעופרת במים אדירים.

[15:10] "You blew with Your wind, the sea covered them; they sank as lead in the mighty waters."

[טו:כג] ויבאו מרתה ולא יכלו לשתת מים ממרה כי מרים הם על כן קרא שמה מרה.

[15:23] And they came to Marah, but they could not drink of the waters of Marah, for they were bitter; therefore, it was named Marah.

TORAH TREASURES • *Beshalach*

[טו:כו] ויאמר אם שמוע תשמע לקול ה' אלקיך והישר בעיניו תעשה והאזנת למצותיו ושמרת כל חקיו כל המחלה אשר שמתי במצרים לא אשים עליך כי אני ה' רפאך.

[15:26] **And He said: "If you will diligently listen to the Voice of Hashem your Lord, and you will do that which is right in His Eyes and will heed to His commandments and keep all His statutes, I will not afflict you with any of the diseases with which I have afflicted the Egyptians; for I am Hashem your Healer."**

... כל המחלה אשר שמתי במצרים לא אשים עליך כי אני ה' רפאך

... I will not afflict you with any of the diseases with which I have afflicted the Egyptians; for I am Hashem your Healer

On the surface, this verse appears self-contradictory. If Hashem will not inflict any diseases on Yisrael, why are they in need of healing?

The suffering that Hashem brought on the Egyptians was intended strictly as retribution and chastisement for enslaving and tormenting the people of Yisrael. By contrast, when Hashem inflicts pain on the people of Yisrael, His purpose is to restore them and heal the spiritual disease of their souls. He prepares the cure in advance of striking the blow. In that, Hashem may be likened to a physician who performs bloodletting or surgery designed to cure the patient. Before beginning his procedure, he prepares the instruments and the medication he will need.

This concept constitutes the underlying meaning of this verse. Hashem promised that He would not afflict the people of Yisrael with the diseases with which He afflicted the Egyptians—as punishment and retribution. And even if He finds it necessary to afflict the people of Yisrael, He will do so only in order to restore their spiritual health, "for I am Hashem your Healer."

Malbim

... כי אני ה' רפאך

... for I am Hashem your Healer

By dividing this phrase into two segments we discover an inspiring new meaning: כי אני ה', *for I am Hashem*, the recognition that

Hashem as the Creator of the Universe, Who with kindness sustains man and His world, this belief, in and of itself רפאך, *is your healer*, provides healing for the stricken body and soul.

Otzar Chaim

. . . ונחנו מה לא עלינו תלונתכם כי על ה'
. . . And what are we? Your complaints are not against us, but against Hashem

This phrase brings to mind a poignant episode that occurred in the synagogue of Rabbi Yonassan Eybeschutz of Prague.

During the *Yom Kippur* service, Rabbi Yonassan noticed a man seated nearby, saying with deep emotion, "I am as mere dust during my lifetime, how much more so after my death." Before long, during the reading of the Torah, the Rabbi observed this same person in a heated argument with the *gabbai*, demanding the honor of being called to the Torah.

Flushed with anger the man exclaimed: "Do you realize who I am and the important office I hold?"

Rabbi Yonassan interjected: "But just a short while ago, you yourself said you were as dust!"

Replied the man: "True indeed. Compared to Hashem I am nothing but dust, but compared to this *gabbai* . . ."

It is this arrogant attitude that prompted our Sages to state that the utterance of Moshe and Aharon is superior to that of Avraham, for when Avraham said, "I am but dust and ashes" (*Beraishis* 18:27) he was addressing Hashem, whereas Moshe's self-effacement was so pervasive that he said, "And what are we?" He considered himself as naught even com-

[טז:ח] ויאמר משה בתת ה' לכם בערב בשר לאכל ולחם בבקר לשבע בשמע ה' את תלנתיכם אשר אתם מלינם עליו ונחנו מה לא עלינו תלנתיכם כי על ה'.

[16:8] And Moshe said: "Hashem will give you meat in the evenings to eat and bread in the mornings to be satiated, for He has heard your complaints against Him. And what are we? Your complaints are not against us, but against Hashem."

TORAH TREASURES • *Beshalach*

[טז:טז] זה הדבר אשר
צוה ה' לקטו ממנו איש
לפי אכלו עמר לגלגלת
מספר נפשתיכם איש
לאשר באהלו תקחו.

[16:16] "This is the thing which Hashem has commanded, to gather of it every man according to his eating, an omer measure for each person, every man shall take according to the number of people in his tent."

pared to those who murmured and complained against Hashem.

Otzar Chaim

זה הדבר . . .
This is the thing . . .

This verse contains all the letters of the *aleph bais*. This unique fact provides an indication for the concept that "whoever upholds the Torah which is written with the 22 letters of the *aleph bais* will be nourished and sustained by Hashem in the same abundant measure and with the same ease as were those who received the manna from heaven."

Otzar Chaim

[טז:כג] ויאמר אלהם
הוא אשר דבר ה' שבתון
שבת קדש לה' מחר את
אשר תאפו אפו ואת אשר
תבשלו בשלו ואת כל
העדף הניחו לכם
למשמרת עד הבקר.

[16:23] And he said to them: "This is what Hashem has spoken. Tomorrow is a day of rest, a holy Sabbath for Hashem. Bake what you must bake, and cook what you must cook, and all that remains store away until the morning."

שבתון שבת קדש לה' מחר . . .
Tomorrow is a day of rest, a holy Sabbath for Hashem . . .

In this verse *Shabbos* is described as *Shabbason Shabbos* whereas in the portion of *Vayakheil* (*ibid.* 35:2) the *Shabbos* is characterized as *Shabbos Shabbason*, reversing the order of the two words. The reason for the variant readings becomes apparent when we consider the commentary of Rabbi David Kimchi (*Redak*).

He states that *Shabbos* denotes the *Shabbos* day itself, while *Shabbason* expresses the idea of *Tosefes Shabbos*, the requirement that we must extend the time of *Shabbos* beyond its limits. Thus, the two phrases in which the word *Shabbos* is alternately preceded and followed by *Shabbason* signify thereby that we must add to the *Shabbos* both at its opening and at its ending.

Traditional

בשלח • TORAH TREASURES

ותן שמה מלא העמר...
and put a full omer measure of manna within it...
The initial letters of the words שמה מלא העמר, *a full omer measure within it*, form the acronym משה, *Moshe*, an allusion to Moshe Rabbeinu in whose merit the manna descended from heaven.

למשמרת לדרתיכם, *for your future generations*. It will endure for all time, for in its merit future generations of the Jewish people will be preserved and find sustenance.

Mahara of Worms

It should be noted that the word שמה, *within it*, consists of the same letters as the name משה, *Moshe*. This being so, the name Moshe appears twice in this passage, as an indication that in Moshe's merit the Jewish people will be nourished and sustained after his demise, as well as during his lifetime.

Chomas Anoch

[טז:לג] ויאמר משה אל אהרן קח צנצנת אחת ותן שמה מלא העמר מן והנח אתו לפני ה' למשמרת לדרתיכם.

[16:33] And Moshe said to Aharon: "Take one jar, and put a full omer measure of manna within it, and store it away before Hashem for your future generations."

...כתב זאת זכרון בספר ושים באזני יהושע כי מחה אמחה את זכר עמלק מתחת השמים
...Write this for a remembrance in the book and bring it to the attention of Yehoshua; for I will utterly blot out the remembrance of Amalek from under the heavens

Even though Hashem commanded that this *mitzvah* be recorded in the *Sefer Torah*, merely writing it would not be enough. In its written form, the word זכר, *remembrance*, could be read as though it were vocalized *zachar*, males, instead of *zecher*, remembrance. This could lead to the erroneous view that only Amalekite males, rather than all of Amalek, must be eradicated.

To avoid this possible error, Hashem com-

[יז:יד] ויאמר ה' אל משה כתב זאת זכרון בספר ושים באזני יהושע כי מחה אמחה את זכר עמלק מתחת השמים.

[17:14] And Hashem said to Moshe: "Write this for a remembrance in the book and bring it to the attention of Yehoshua; for I will utterly blot out the remembrance of Amalek from under the heavens."

manded Moshe to transmit the *mitzvah* orally to Yehoshua by enunciating the word, with its correct pronunciation, thereby denoting that any remembrance of Amalek is to be utterly destroyed.

Vilna Gaon

Yisro / יתרו

ויספר משה לחתנו את כל אשר עשה ה' לפרעה ולמצרים על אודת ישראל . . .

And Moshe told his father-in-law all that Hashem had done to Pharaoh and to the Egyptians concerning Yisrael . . .

Rabbi Chaim Vital, commenting on this verse, writes that the Egyptians might have viewed the plagues as an expression of divine wrath at Pharaoh's rebellious and scornful attitude towards Hashem, as revenge for Pharaoh's contemptuous statements, such as "I do not know Hashem" or "Who is Hashem that I should listen to Him?" They might have reasoned that a more respectful attitude on the part of Pharaoh could have led to a compromise with Hashem under which the people of Yisrael would have remained their slaves, albeit with better working conditions. In their view, the Exodus with the plagues might have been Hashem's retribution for the insult to His dignity.

The truth, however, was that Hashem performed the miracles of the Exodus, not for His

[יח:ח] ויספר משה לחתנו את כל אשר עשה ה' לפרעה ולמצרים על אודת ישראל את כל התלאה אשר מצאתם בדרך ויצלם ה'.

[18:8] **And Moshe told his father-in-law all that Hashem had done to Pharaoh and to the Egyptians concerning Yisrael, all the hardship that had come upon them by the way, and how Hashem had delivered them.**

TORAH TREASURES • *Yisro*

own sake, but solely for the sake of Yisrael. This becomes evident in the way He saved them from the onslaught of the pursuing Egyptians and from Amalek, in His protective Clouds of Glory, the manna, etc.

All this is implied in the verse. "And Moshe told his father-in-law all that Hashem had done to Pharaoh and to the Egyptians concerning Yisrael"—exclusively for their sake, and not because of Pharaoh's disrespect. Proof of Hashem's boundless love for Yisrael existed in "all the hardship that had come upon them by the way, and how Hashem had delivered them."

Nachal Kedumim

In a similar vein, Maharam ben Chaviv explains the reason that the people of Yisrael sang Hashem's praises only after the parting of the *Yam Suf* (Sea of Reeds), rather than after witnessing the miracles of the Exodus. It was only after the parting of the *Yam Suf* that it became clear to all the world that the miracles of the Exodus had been performed for the sake of Hashem's love of Israel and not as a penalty for Pharaoh's denial of Hashem.

This is expressed in the words אז ישיר משה, *Moshe then sang;* only then and not before, because until that moment the world might still have been under the mistaken impression that the Exodus was Hashem's revenge for Pharaoh's insults.

Chomas Anoch

[יח:יא] עתה ידעתי כי גדול ה' מכל האלקים כי בדבר אשר זדו עליהם.

[18:11] "Now I know that Hashem is great-

... כי בדבר אשר זדו עליהם

... for their own plots turned against them

Rashi explains this verse to mean they received the same punishment that they themselves had meted out. They had drowned the Jewish children, and now, *quid pro quo*, they themselves were drowned.

The Baal Shem Tov finds in this verse a universal concept that transcends its literal meaning. People are punished according to the sentence they themselves decree. The underlying lesson is that a person is quick to pass judgment on a fellow man who is guilty of wrongdoing, and in his mind, he determines the punishment that would be fitting and just. In so doing, he is actually passing his own sentence, for he forgets that he, too, is not altogether blameless.

Pardes Yosef

er than all deities, for their own plots turned against them."

[יח:טז] כי יהיה להם דבר בא אלי ושפטתי בין איש ובין רעהו והודעתי את חקי האלקים ואת תורתיו.

[18:16] "When they have a dispute, he comes to me, and I judge between each man and his fellow man, and I let them know the statutes of the Lord and His laws.

כי יהיה להם דבר בא אלי ...
When they have a dispute, he comes to me . . .

Since the word להם, *they have*, is in the plural, we would expect, correspondingly, to read באו אלי, *they come to me*, also in the plural, rather than the word that actually appears, בא אלי, *he comes to me*.

In bygone days, questions concerning finances were considered in the same category as questions of dietary law. In either case, the questioner relied on the rabbi for *Halachic* guidance. Both parties in a financial dispute recoiled from the thought of acquiring the slightest amount that was not rightfully theirs, and consequently, there was no need for both parties to appear before the court. Either one of them could present his own case as well as that of his opponent with total objectivity.

Likewise, if a person caused damage to his fellow man's property, he did not have to be summoned into court. He himself would ask the judge what amount he owed the injured

TORAH TREASURES • *Yisro*

party according to *Halachah*, and he would voluntarily pay the assessed damages. This high-minded outlook is reflected in the singular form of בא אלי, *he comes to me*. Only one of the litigants went to Moshe, representing both parties.

Malbim

[יט:ב] ויסעו מרפידים ויבאו מדבר סיני ויחנו במדבר ויחן שם ישראל נגד ההר.

[19:2] **And they departed from Refidim and came to the Sinai Desert, and they made camp in the desert, and Yisrael encamped there before the mountain.**

... ויחן שם ישראל נגד ההר

... and Yisrael encamped there before the mountain

One of the epithets for the *yetzer hora*, the evil inclination, is הר, *mountain*. For example, the *Gemara* in *Chagigah* states that to the righteous, the *yetzer hora* will appear as a mountain.

It is the primary aim of the *yetzer hora* to sow dissension and discord among the people of Yisrael. The exact opposite sentiment, that of unity, prevailed at the time of the Stand at Mount Sinai. Yisrael was united in purpose and spirit as never before.

This is reflected in the singular form of ויחן שם, *and he encamped*, instead of ויחנו שם, *and they encamped*. As Rashi remarks, they were united, as one man, with one heart. נגד ההר, *before the mountain*, arrayed against the aims and aspirations of the *yetzer hora*, the evil inclination.

Rabbi Nosson Adler

[יט:י] ויאמר ה' אל משה לך אל העם וקדשתם היום ומחר וכבסו שמלתם.

[19:10] **And Hashem said to Moshe: "Go to the nation and sanctify them today and**

... לך אל העם וקדשתם היום ומחר

Go to the nation and sanctify them today and tomorrow ...

Homiletically, this verse can be interpreted as teaching a strategy for overcoming the seductive voice of the *yetzer hora*, the evil inclination.

The *yetzer hora* entices a person, telling him, "Just succumb to my temptations today; tomorrow you can sanctify yourself!" But the person must respond, "Waiting until tomorrow will not do; we must sanctify ourselves today and not wait until tomorrow."

Bais Avraham

אנכי ה' אלקיך . . .
I am Hashem your Lord . . .
The ten commandments are comprised of a total of 620 letters, which corresponds to the 613 *Mitzvos d'Oraysa*, Torah statutes, supplemented by 7 *Mitzvos d'Rabbanan*, Rabbinic precepts, totalling 620.

This equation expresses the notion that all *mitzvos* are included within the ten commandments and can be derived from them. The *Avudarham* notes that the numerical value of the sentence ה' מלך, ה' מלך, ה' ימלוך לעולם ועד, *Hashem reigns, Hashem has reigned, Hashem shall reign for all eternity*, equals the numerical value of כתר, *crown*, also 620.

Thus, the number 620 symbolizes the concept that Hashem's *mitzvos* are the foundation of His sovereignty, and by our acceptance of His *mitzvos* we proclaim Him the Supreme Ruler of the Universe.

Nachal Kedumim

Author's note:
It should be noted that *gematria* is based on the *kri*, the words according to their spoken sound. (See Rabbeinu Eliyahu Mizrachi in Bamidbar 15:39.)

[כ:ב] אנכי ה' אלקיך אשר הוצאתיך מארץ מצרים מבית עבדים.

[20:2] I am Hashem your Lord who brought you out of the land of Egypt, from the house of bondage.

. . . אשר הוצאתיך מארץ מצרים
. . . who brought you out of the land of Egypt

TORAH TREASURES • *Yisro*

The numerical value of אשר, *Who*, equals that of דצ"ך עד"ש באח"ב, Rabbi Yehudah's mnemonic device, combining the initial letters of each plague into the famous acronym mentioned in the *Haggadah*.

In light of this *gematria*, the verse can be translated as "אשר brought you out," meaning the combined impact of the ten plagues brought about the Exodus from Egypt.

Nachal Kedumim

[כ:ח-ט] זכור את יום השבת לקדשו. ששת ימים תעבד ועשית כל מלאכתך.

[20:8-9] Remember the Sabbath day to keep it holy. Six days shall you labor and do all your work.

זכור את יום השבת לקדשו. ששת ימים תעבד . . .
Remember the Sabbath day to keep it holy. Six days shall you labor . . .

On the surface, these verses appear to be two independent statements, both referring to *Shabbos*.

The Vilna Gaon, viewing these verses from the perspective of *Halachah*, establishes a logical correlation between them. The *Gemara* in *Shabbos* 69b teaches that if one is traveling through a desert and does not remember which day is *Shabbos*, he should count six days from that point and observe the seventh day as *Shabbos*. Nevertheless, in the opinion of Rava, on each of these days he is permitted to perform only the minimum amount of work essential for his sustenance, but not more.

Predicated on this *Gemara*, the two verses can be seen as closely linked.

"Remember the *Shabbos* to keep it holy." Wherever you travel be sure to remember on what day *Shabbos* falls. "Six days shall you labor and do all your work," for if you know on what day *Shabbos* occurs, you may labor during the other six days as much as you wish. Should you lose track of the days, however, then you may not do "all your work" during the

יתרו • TORAH TREASURES

six days you have counted. You may only do the minimum work required for your livelihood.

Iturei Torah

ששת ימים תעבד ועשית כל מלאכתך . . .
Six days shall you labor and do all your work . . .

Rashi comments that when the *Shabbos* comes a person should feel as though all his work is completed. Alternatively, Rashi's comment can be translated as "it will be in your eyes as though all your work were completed."

According to this translation, our verse implies the inherent promise that resting on *Shabbos* will never lead to monetary loss. The work left undone because of *Shabbos* will be compensated with rich heavenly blessings of success.

A similar idea is expressed in the beginning of *Tehillim*. David Hamelech, in praise of the perfect Jew, proclaims: "And in His Law he meditates day and night . . . and in whatever he does he shall prosper."

David Hamelech declares that a student of Torah will suffer no deprivation. Despite days and nights spent in Torah study, he will never lack worldly goods.

Hashem will bestow His abundant blessings on the Torah student and the *Shabbos* observer alike.

Panim Yafos

כבד את אביך ואת אמך . . .
Honor your father and your mother . . .

The *Zohar* teaches that with every *mitzvah* a person performs, the souls of his departed parents are given an added degree of spiritual

[כ:ח-ט] זכור את יום השבת לקדשו. ששת ימים תעבד ועשית כל מלאכתך.

[20:8-9] Remember the Sabbath day to keep it holy. Six days shall you labor and do all your work.

[כ:יב] כבד את אביך ואת אמך למען יארכון ימיך על האדמה אשר ה' אלקיך נתן לך.

[20:12] Honor your father and your mother in order that your days may be long upon the land which Hashem your Lord gives you.

stature and glory in Gan Eden.

Moreover, we learn that as a result of this ascent there is a threefold reward from Heaven for his *mitzvah*—the reward for the *mitzvah* itself, the fulfillment of the *mitzvah* of honoring a father and the *mitzvah* of honoring a mother.

In light of this passage of the *Zohar*, the author of the famous work *Yesod Veshoresh Ha'avodah* would recite the *Kabbalistic* declaration of intent *Leshaim Yichud* three times before performing any *mitzvah*, in recognition of the threefold character of the *mitzvah*.

Memayanos Hanetzach

[כ:יב] כבד את אביך ואת אמך למען יארכון ימיך על האדמה אשר ה' אלקיך נתן לך.

[20:12] Honor your father and your mother in order that your days may be long upon the land which Hashem your Lord gives you.

כבד את אביך ואת אמך ...

Honor your father and your mother ...

The story is told of a man who approached Rabbi Chaim Soloveitchik with the following query:

His father, who lived in a faraway city, was not feeling well. In order to comply with the mitzvah of כיבוד אב, *honoring one's father*, he felt it was his duty to travel there in order to visit him on his sickbed.

Inasmuch as the *Halachah* explicitly states that all expenditure incurred in fulfillment of this *mitzvah* are paid by the father, and since his travel expenses would be considerable, he wanted to know whether under these circumstances he would be exempt from making this visit.

Rabbi Chaim replied briskly: "True indeed, you are exempt from traveling by train. Therefore, go there on foot."

Memayanos Hanetzach

לא תרצח ...
Do not murder ...

When the Ten Commandments are read in public, לא תרצח, *do not murder*, is vocalized with the vowel *kametz* as *sirtzuch*, but when they are read privately it is pronounced with the vowel *patach* as *sirtzach*. Grammatically, the variant readings are the result of the respective use of the upper and lower cantillation (*taam ha'elyon* and *taam hatachton*). In the upper cantillation, each commandment is read as a separate sentence; in the lower, they are arranged as one single sentence.

Some commentators find in the different readings an expression of two aspects of murder.

On the one hand, there is murder in its literal sense, the destruction of life by bloodshed. This flagrant or open form of murder is described by *sirtzach* with a *patach*, *patach* being a form of the verb "to open."

By contrast, humiliating one's fellow man in public constitutes a more subtle form of murder. As stated in *Gemara Bava Metzia* 58b, "Shaming one's fellow man in public is tantamount to spilling his blood" (since the blood drains from his face).

This figurative form of murder is indicated by *sirtzuch* with a *kametz*, *kametz* being a form of the verb "to squeeze." The blood is squeezed and drawn from the face of the humiliated person.

The crime of actual murder is punishable even when committed in private. Therefore, when this verse is read privately, it is read with a *patach* indicating actual flagrant murder. On the other hand, the figurative form of murder through humiliation is punishable

[כ:יג-טז] לא תרצח. לא תנאף. לא תגנב. לא תענה ברעך עד שקר.

[20:13-16] Do not murder. Do not commit adultery. Do not steal. Do not bear false witness against your neighbor.

TORAH TREASURES • *Yisro*

only when committed in public. Thus, when the verse is read in public, it is read with a *kametz*.

Otzar Chaim

[כ:כ] לא תעשון אתי אלהי כסף ואלהי זהב לא תעשו לכם.
[20:23] You shall not make anything beside Me; you shall not make for yourselves silver deities or gold deities.

לא תעשון אתי אלהי כסף ואלהי זהב לא תעשו לכם
You shall not make anything beside Me; you shall not make for yourselves silver deities or gold deities

This verse can also be read as saying: "When you are beside Me, meaning when you stand before Me engrossed in prayer, do not allow your thoughts to dwell on your possessions of silver and gold. I will regard the harboring of such unworthy thoughts as serious a sin as the making of idols of silver and gold."

Rabbeinu Bachya

[כ:כד] מזבח אדמה תעשה לי וזבחת עליו את עלתיך ואת שלמיך את צאנך ואת בקרך בכל המקום אשר אזכיר את שמי אבוא אליך וברכתיך.
[20:24] You shall make an earthen altar for Me, and you shall sacrifice upon it your burnt offerings and your peace offerings, your sheep and your oxen; in every place where I cause My name to be mentioned I will come to you and bless you.

... אבוא אליך וברכתיך
... I will come to you and bless you

The numerical value of אבוא, *I will come*, equals 10, as if to say, "Wherever I will find ten men engaged in prayer I will come to you and bless you."

Baal Haturim

Mishpatim / משפטים

ואם אמר יאמר העבד . . .
But if the servant shall plainly say . . .

The *Midrash* tells us that Moshe metaphorically presented the above verse as he pleaded with Hashem to be admitted to Eretz Yisrael.

Moshe exclaimed: "I love my master," meaning Hashem, "my wife," meaning the Torah and "my children," meaning the people of Yisrael. "I will not go free," meaning I do not want to be separated from any one of them.

To which Hashem replied: "Speak no more to Me of this matter." (*Devarim* 3:26)

Rabbi Yehoshua Leib Diskin offers an illuminating interpretation of this dialogue.

Moshe, the supreme expert on Torah law, knew full well that this claim was irrefutable, and that when confronted with this argument, Hashem would be compelled to grant him permission to enter the Land. However, the *Gemara* in *Kiddushin* stipulates that in order for the servant's claim to be valid he must repeat it, as indicated by the double use of אמר, *say*, in this verse. Moshe's plea would

[כא:ה] ואם אמר יאמר העבד אהבתי את אדני את אשתי ואת בני לא אצא חפשי.

[21:5] But if the servant shall plainly say: "I love my master, my wife and my children; I will not go out free."

TORAH TREASURES • *Mishpatim*

indeed have been accepted had he repeated it, but Hashem silenced him saying, "Speak no more to Me of this matter."

Rabbi Chaim Soloveitchik

[כא:ו] והגישו אדניו אל האלהים והגישו אל הדלת או אל המזוזה ורצע אדניו את אזנו במרצע ועבדו לעלם.

[21:6] Then his master shall bring him to the court, and he shall bring him near to the door or to the door post, and his master shall bore his ear with an awl and he shall serve him forever.

... ורצע אדניו את אזנו במרצע
... and his master shall bore his ear with an awl

Why with an awl? Because the numerical value of מרצע, *awl*, equals 400. What is the significance of the number 400?

Hashem redeemed us from 400 years of bondage for the expressed purpose of making us His servants, as it is written, כי לי בני ישראל עבדים, *"For the people of Yisrael are My servants."* (*Vayikra* 25:55) Now this person goes and acquires his own master; let him be afflicted with a מרצע, *awl*, which numerically equals 400.

Daas Zekeinim Mibaalei Hatosefos

[כא:יא] ואם שלש אלה לא יעשה לה ויצאה חנם אין כסף.

[21:11] And if he does not do these three things for her, then she shall she go out without compensation, without money.

... ויצאה חנם אין כסף
... then she shall go out without compensation, without money

The last letters of the words ויצאה חנם אין, *then she shall go out without*, form the acronym of the name המן, *Haman*.

Haman gained the right to persecute the Jewish people "without compensation, without money," without having to pay for it, as it is written, "The silver is given to you, the people also, to do with them as you see fit." (*Esther* 3:11) Hashem foiled Haman's plan and saved the Jewish people likewise "without compensation, without money," in consonance with the words of *Yeshayah* 52:3: "For thus says Hashem: You were sold for nought and you shall be redeemed without money."

Chomas Anoch

משפטים • TORAH TREASURES

... והאלקים אנה לידו ושמתי לך מקום
... yet the Lord caused it to happen, then I will designate for you a place

The initial letters of the words אנה לידו ושמתי לך, *caused it to happen, then I will designate for you*, form the acronym אלול, *Elul*, the month dedicated to the preparation for *Yamim Noraim*, the Days of Awe.

Finding an allusion to the month of Elul in these particular words is an indication that during this month Hashem grants forgiveness to anyone who inadvertently committed a sin throughout the year.

Yalkut Reuveini

[כא:יג] ואשר לא צדה והאלקים אנה לידו ושמתי לך מקום אשר ינוס שמה.

[21:13] But if he did not lie in wait, yet the Lord caused it to happen, then I will designate for you a place to which he may flee.

... ומכה אביו ואמו
And he who strikes his father or his mother ...

Rabbi Shlomo Eiger writes in his work *Gilyon Maharsha* that it is advisable for an adult person who during childhood struck his father to take upon himself certain voluntary obligations so as to atone for his transgression.

Similarly, Rabbi Klonymos Kalman of Krakow states in his work *Ma'or Vashamesh* that the saintly Rabbi Elimelech of Lizhensk repented for the sins of his early youth and even for the discomfort he caused his mother while he was still in her womb.

Memayanos Hanetzach

[כא:טו] ומכה אביו ואמו מות יומת.

[21:15] And he who strikes his father or his mother shall surely be put to death.

... ורפא ירפא
... and provide for him to be thoroughly healed

The question arises: If it is Hashem's Will that a person becomes ill, may he actively seek relief from his sickness by going to a physician? Our Sages find the answer based in the abovementioned verse. " ... for him to be

[כא:יט] אם יקום והתהלך בחוץ על משענתו ונקה המכה רק שבתו יתן ורפא ירפא.

[21:19] If he rises and walks outside on his own strength, then he that struck

TORAH TREASURES • *Mishpatim*

him be acquitted; only, he shall pay for the loss of his work and provide for him to be thoroughly healed.

thoroughly healed." This teaches us that a physician has the right to practice medicine.

The Chozeh of Lublin adds an important corollary to this ruling. He states that a physician is restricted to practicing the art of restoring health; he does not have the right to declare a patient's status hopeless or terminal. He has neither the competence nor the qualifications to make such judgments. Life and death are in Hashem's Hands alone.

The Chozeh of Lublin

[כא:כא] אך אם יום או יומים יעמד לא יקם כי כספו הוא.

[21:21] **However, if he survives for a day or two, he shall not be avenged, for he is his property.**

אך אם יום או יומים יעמד לא יקם כי כספו הוא
However, if he survives for a day or two, he shall not be avenged, for he is his property

Rabbi Mahara Chiyvun in his work *Amaros Tehoros* discusses the case of a person who did *teshuvah*, who sincerely repented of his sin, but subsequently reverted to his old ways. Does his lapse cancel his prior repentance, and as a result, is his old sin reinstated? Or does his previous repentance and forgiveness still stand?

After pondering this question, he reached a conclusion. The determining factor is the person's attitude towards his previous *teshuvah*. If, upon reverting to his sinful ways, he has become so debased that he regrets ever having repented, then his prior sin is revived. On the other hand, if he momentarily succumbed to temptation but in his heart he still adheres to his earlier repentance, then his repentance remains intact and his old sin remains forgiven.

Our verse hints at this concept: אך אם יום או יומים, *however, if for a day or two*, referring to the one day of *Yom Kippur*, and the two days of *Rosh Hashannah*, יעמד, *he survives* or

180

maintains his *teshuvah*, but then he backslides, לא יקם, *he shall not be avenged* or punished for his old sin, כי כספו הוא, *for he still desires* his previous repentance (translating the word כסף according to the alternate verb form which means to yearn or to desire). He only sinned because he could not withstand temptation, but since in his heart he stands by his repentance, his old sin remains forgiven.

Chomas Anoch

עין תחת עין ...
An eye for an eye ...

[כא:כד] עין תחת עין שן תחת שן יד תחת יד רגל תחת רגל.
[21:24] An eye for an eye, a tooth for a tooth, a hand for a hand, a foot for a foot.

The *Gemara* in *Bava Kama* 84a teaches that this passage is not to be applied in its literal sense. Instead, the true meaning of "an eye for an eye" is the right to monetary compensation for the loss of an eye, tooth or limb.

A truly amazing allusion, concealed in the words עין תחת עין, *an eye for an eye*, confirms this legal principle.

If we arrange the letters of the *aleph bais* in a vertical row we find that underneath the letters of the word עין the letters פכס appear. The letters פכס, rearranged, form the word כסף, *money*. The phrase עין תחת עין can thus be rendered as follows: עין, for an injury to an eye, one must pay תחת עין, that which is תחת, *underneath*, the letters עין, namely כסף, *money*.

Vilna Gaon

וכי יפתח איש בור או כי יכרה איש בר ...
And if a man shall open a pit, or if a man shall dig a pit. . .

[כא:לג] וכי יפתח איש בור או כי יכרה איש בר ולא יכסנו ונפל שמה שור או חמור.
[21:33] And if a man shall open a pit, or if

In this verse, the word בור, *pit*, occurs two times. The first time it appears in its full form,

TORAH TREASURES • *Mishpatim*

a man shall dig a pit and not cover it, and an ox or a donkey shall fall into it.

with a ו, *vav*. The second time it appears in the abbreviated form, without a *vav*. This incongruity can be explained in light of the applicable laws.

The *Halachah* states that a person who opens a pit is liable only if the pit has a depth of 10 handbreadths. By contrast, if a person digs a pit to a depth of nine handbreadths, and then another man digs an additional handbreadth completing the pit to ten handbreadths, only the latter is liable. (*Bava Kama* 51a)

Thus, in connection with opening a pit, the word בור is spelled in its full form to indicate that he is liable only if the pit has already been completed to the prescribed depth of ten handbreadths. In the case of digging a pit, it is spelled in its incomplete form, hinting at the second digger's liability, even though he only dug a partial, incomplete pit.

Vilna Gaon

[כב:כא] כל אלמנה ויתום לא תענון.

[22:21] **You shall not afflict any widow or orphan.**

כל אלמנה ויתום לא תענון
You shall not afflict any widow or orphan

Shortly before *Pesach*, Rabbi Yisrael Salanter was forced to set out on an extended journey, which made it impossible for him to oversee the baking of the *shemurah matzoh* for his personal use.

His students gladly volunteered to fulfill the task of supervising the baking, pledging the observance of the most rigorous strictures. When they asked Rabbi Yisrael as to what particular aspect of the baking process required their most intense scrutiny, he replied:

"Pay attention to the widow who kneads the dough. It is forbidden to rush her or drive her, even though kneading the dough quickly is the superb way of performing the *mitzvah* in that it prevents the slightest danger of leavening."

After a brief pause, he continued: "The highest degree of *kashrus* of the *matzos* is achieved not only by the observance of all the laws of *Pesach*, but also by the pertinent laws of the *Choshen Mishpat*, the Code of Civil Law."

Memayanos Hanetzach

אם ענה תענה אתו . . .
If you persecute him . . .

The *Gemara* in *Bava Basra* enlightens us as to the true relationship that existed between Chanah and Peninah.

According to our Sages, when Peninah "angered her deeply to make her fret" (*Shmuel I* 1:6), she did so for the purest of motives. Her aim was to induce Chanah to beg Hashem for children. The *Gemara* concludes that in spite of her commendable intentions, Peninah was punished for the anguish she inflicted on Chanah, her penalty being the death of her children. The lesson inherent in this *Gemara* is that "the end does not justify the means."

This lesson is implicit in the abovementioned verse. אם ענה תענה אתו, *if you persecute him*, an unfortunate person, albeit for the most commendable reasons, צעק יצעק אלי, to make him *cry out to me*, it is, nonetheless, an evil deed on your part. שמע אשמע צעקתו, *I will surely hear his cry*, וחרה אפי, *my anger will be inflamed* and you will be punished.

Vilna Gaon

[כב:כב] אם ענה תענה אתו כי אם צעק יצעק אלי שמע אשמע צעקתו.

[22:22] **If you persecute him in any way so that he cries out to Me, I will surely hear his cry.**

אם כסף תלוה את עמי את העני עמך . . .
If you lend money to any of My people, to the poor among you . . .

TORAH TREASURES • Mishpatim

In this verse we can find an allusion to two rabbinic sayings. First, it is forbidden to lend money, except in the presence of witnesses. (The *Gemara* explains that this rule is for the protection of the lender, for in the event he tries to collect an unwitnessed loan and the borrower denies having borrowed from him, the lender will appear dishonest, and he will be denounced and cursed by one and all.) Second, charity should be given in private, so as not to shame the recipient. Both these statements can be traced to a variant reading of the abovementioned verse.

אם כסף תלוה, *if you lend money*, את עמי, *do so in the presence of my people*, that is to say, in front of witnesses. However, את העני, when you give charity *to the poor*, do so עמך, *with you*, alone, that is to say, in secret, with no one present but you and the needy person.

Nachal Kedumim

[כב:כד] אם כסף תלוה את עמי את העני עמך לא תהיה לו כנשה לא תשימון עליו נשך.

[22:24] **If you lend money to any of My people, to the poor among you, you shall not be as a creditor towards him, nor shall you impose interest upon him.**

... את העני עמך

... to the poor among you

It is written in *Tehillim*: אשרי שומרי משפט עושה צדקה בכל עת. "*Fortunate are those who preserve justice, who does righteousness at all times.*"

Upon closer inspection of this verse we note that שומרי משפט, *those who preserve justice*, is written in the plural, whereas עושה צדקה, *who does righteousness*, is in the singular.

The reason for this disparity can be traced to the inherent difference between the *mitzvah* of *tzedakah*, giving charity, and other *mitzvos*.

The performance of all *mitzvos* should be accompanied by a public manifestation of our devotion to Hashem and our love of His commandments. The exception is the *mitzvah* of *tzedakah*, which should be performed in private, in strict confidence, without public fanfare. Indeed, the highest form of *tzedakah* is *mattan besaiser*, anonymous giving.

This difference is reflected in the verse in *Tehillim*. *Fortunate are those who preserve justice*, those who gather in great multitudes (in the plural) so as to observe the *mitzvos* publicly and preserve justice; but the one *who does righteousness*, who gives charity discreetly (in the singular) behind closed doors, he gives charity *at all times*. For one who seeks public acclaim performs *mitzvos* only when others are watching, whereas one who gives charity in secret does so constantly.

This thought is expressed in the abovementioned verse את העני עמך, *to the poor among you*. Charity is strictly between you and the needy person.

Ksav Sofer

אם כסף תלוה את עמי את העני עמך ...
If you lend money to any of My people, to the poor among you ...

A mighty potentate one day asked his wealthy chancellor: "Tell me, what is the value of your possessions?"

Without hesitation, the chancellor replied: "The value of all my assets amounts to 30,000 dinars."

The potentate angrily responded: "Why do you lie to me? Your many ships that sail the seven seas, loaded with silks and spices from the Orient, are worth many times the 30,000 dinars you mentioned. And what about your huge treasure houses filled with gold and jewels?"

[כב:כד] אם כסף תלוה את עמי את העני עמך לא תהיה לו כנשה לא תשימון עליו נשך.

[22:24] **If you lend money to any of My people, to the poor among you, you shall not be as a creditor towards him, nor shall you impose interest upon him.**

TORAH TREASURES • *Mishpatim*

The chancellor humbly explained: "Your majesty, you asked me about the extent of my wealth, and I answered truthfully. For what I really possess are the 30,000 dinars. This is the amount I distributed to the poor; this amount I can truly call mine. All my ships and warehouses do not really belong to me, for I may lose it all tomorrow."

Our verse alludes to this concept. אם כסף תלוה, *if you lend money to any of My people,* את העני, *to the poor,* עמך, *these are the things that will remain with you.*

Nachal Kedumim

[כג:ג] ודל לא תהדר בריבו

[23:3] **Nor shall you favor the pauper in his dispute.**

ודל לא תהדר בריבו
Nor shall you favor the pauper in his dispute

The word בריבו, *in his dispute,* alludes to the issue the poor man raises with Hashem. He argues: "Why does Hashem provide sustenance for all, while I am without food or clothing?"

When a person gives charity he weakens the poor man's claim against Hashem. Conversely, when a person refrains from giving charity the poor man's arguments are reinforced. This verse expresses Hashem's command to us not to favor or reinforce the poor man's argument to Hashem. On the contrary, we are to assist him by extending a helping hand.

Ohr Hachaim

[כג:ד-ה] כי תפגע שור איבך או חמרו תעה השב תשיבנו לו. כי תראה חמור שנאך רבץ תחת משאו וחדלת מעזב לו עזב תעזב עמו.

[23:4-5] **If you encounter your en- counter your en-**

כי תפגע שור איבך או חמרו . . .
If you encounter your enemy's ox or his donkey . . .

The following passage in *Devarim* 22:1-4 closely parallels these verses: "You shall not see your brother's ox or his sheep driven away and hide yourself from them; you shall surely bring them back to your brother... You shall not see your brother's donkey or his ox fallen down by the wayside and hide yourself from them; you shall surely help him lift them up again."

The verses in *Devarim* differ from these verses in one significant point. In these verses, the object is "your *enemy's* ox," whereas in *Devarim* the verses refer to "your *brother's* donkey" and "your *brother's* ox."

What is the meaning of the shift in the wording from enemy to brother?

The *Gemara* in *Pesachim* 113b comments that "the enemy" in *Mishpatim* refers to a Jewish foe. But is it permitted, the *Gemara* asks, to hate a fellow Jew? Yes, the *Gemara* replies, if he committed a sinful act. In that case, it is permitted to hate him.

These verses appear before the *chet ha'egel*, the sin of the golden calf idol, when all the people of Yisrael were in an elevated state of being, described as a "kingdom of priests" and "a holy nation." Then, it was permissible to hate an individual who sinned.

However, after the *chet ha'egel*, the people of Yisrael fell from this high spiritual level. Then, if a person witnessed a sinful act, he would examine his own conduct and find that he himself was not perfect either. This being so, he was not permitted to hate a fellow Jew who had gone astray, since only a saintly person, who himself is righteous and pure has the right to hate a sinner.

Thus, these verses tell us that even an enemy must be helped with his animal, but in *Devarim* there are no longer any "enemies," only "brothers."

Meshech Chochmah

emy's ox or his donkey going astray, you shall surely bring it back to him again. If you see your enemy's donkey sprawled under its burden you shall surely help him unload it.

TORAH TREASURES • *Mishpatim*

[כג:ז] מדבר שקר תרחק
ונקי וצדיק אל תהרג כי
לא אצדיק רשע.

[23:7] **Distance yourself from a false matter, and do not kill the innocent and the righteous, for I will not justify the wicked.**

[כג:ח] ושחד לא תקח כי
השחד יעור פקחים ויסלף
דברי צדיקים.

[23:8] **And you shall not take a bribe, for bribery blinds the clearsighted and perverts the words of the righteous.**

מדבר שקר תרחק ...
Distance yourself from a false matter ...

Rabbi Zisha suggests the following translation: "מדבר שקר, *because of every untrue word you utter,* תרחק, *you grow more distant from Hashem,*" for it is written: "A liar shall not stand in front of His Eyes."

Otzar Chaim

ושחד לא תקח ...
And you shall not take a bribe ...

The Hebrew word for bribe is שחד. In the sequence of the *aleph bais* we find that the letters that follow the letters ש-ח-ד yield the word תטה, *you will be inclined, bend, deviate.* By accepting a bribe, a judge will surely *be inclined* to rule in favor of the person who gave the bribe, will *bend* the law and *deviate* from the path of true justice.

Chomas Anoch

ושחד לא תקח כי השחד יעור פקחים ...
And you shall not take a bribe, for bribery blinds the clearsighted ...

The *Midrash* tells us that Yitzchak's eyes were blinded because he accepted a bribe from his son Eisav, notwithstanding the fact that Eisav was duty bound to honor his father. We can infer from this *Midrash* that this verse is to be taken literally, that the acceptance of a bribe causes blindness.

What is the connection between blindness and taking a bribe? A possible answer is suggested by the words of the author of the *Urim Vetumim,* who never responded to any *Halachic* inquiry without first reviewing it in the major works of *Halachah,* because as he writes, *"Osiyos machkimos,* viewing the letters impart wisdom." Only by reading the original text (and not by relying on your memory) can you arrive at the truth.

Based on these words, we may conclude that blindness is indeed a suitable punishment for accepting a bribe. A judge needs his eyes to study and arrive at a true ruling, but a judge who accepts bribes and does not search for the truth has no need for his eyes.

Bais Pinchas

... נעשה ונשמע
... we will do and we will heed

The *Massorah* links this phrase with two other seemingly unrelated phrases, all containing the word ונשמע, *and we will listen or heed.* The second is in *Shemos* (28:35): ונשמע קולו בבאו אל הקודש, *And the sound (of the bells) shall be heard when he goes into the holy place.* The third is in *Megillas Esther* (1:20): ונשמע פתגם המלך, *And the king's decree shall be heard.*

How are these passages interconnected?

An answer may be gleaned from the *Gemara* in *Shabbos* 88a which expounds the verse "And they stood at the foot of the mountain." (*Shemos* 19:17). The *Gemara* tells us that at the time of *Mattan Torah,* the giving of the Torah, Hashem uprooted the mountain from its place, held it over their heads like a cask and said: "If you do not accept the Torah, this will be your gravesite." Rashi explains that this statement provides the people of Yisrael with a powerful argument concerning the Torah; if at a future date, Hashem will bring them to justice for having violated the laws they agreed to uphold, they can then argue that they

[כד:ז] ויקח ספר הברית ויקרא באזני העם ויאמרו כל אשר דבר ה' נעשה ונשמע.

[24:7] And he took the book of the covenant, and read in the hearing of the people, and they said: "All that Hashem has spoken we will do and we will heed."

TORAH TREASURES • *Mishpatim*

[כד:ז] ויקח ספר הברית ויקרא באזני העם ויאמרו כל אשר דבר ה' נעשה ונשמע.

[24:7] **And he took the book of the covenant, and read in the hearing of the people, and they said: "All that Hashem has spoken we will do and we will heed."**

accepted the Torah under duress.

The Rashba writes that this defense was valid only until they entered Eretz Yisrael. After their entry it was no longer valid since their presence in the land was conditional upon their acceptance of the Torah, as it is written: "He gave them the lands of the nations in order that they keep His statutes."

However, when they were sent into exile, the argument held true again. In spite of that, they willingly accepted the Torah in the days of Achashverus. This evolution from forced acceptance of Hashem's Torah is alluded to in this *Massorah*.

Even though they had declared, נעשה ונשמע, *We will do and we will heed*, Hashem held the mountain over their heads, forcing them into accepting the Torah and providing them with a strong defense.

This defense, however, was not for all times. Upon entering Eretz Yisrael it lost its legal effect, as indicated in the verse, translated figuratively: ונשמע קולו בבאו אל הקודש, *The Voice of Hashem will be obeyed voluntarily upon our entering the Holy Land*.

Still, when they were sent into exile, the basis for the voluntary acceptance was nullified, and the original defense once again became valid. Nevertheless, in the days of Achashverus they willingly and voluntarily declared their allegiance to Hashem and His Torah, as is expressed in the passage in *Megillas Esther*, again translated figuratively: ונשמע פתגם המלך, *And the decree of the Almighty King was heard and accepted*.

Chida

Terumah / תרומה

[כה:ב] דבר אל בני ישראל ויקחו לי תרומה מאת כל איש אשר ידבנו לבו תקחו את תרומתי.

[25:2] **Speak to the people of Yisrael, and let them take for Me an offering; from every man whose heart makes him willing shall you take My offering.**

ויקחו לי תרומה . . .
and let them take for Me an offering . . .

This verse alludes to an easy method to facilitate the fulfillment of the *mitzvah* of *tzedakah*. It is to establish a *tzedakah* account into which to deposit those funds assigned to charity. Then, whenever a needy person or organization solicits *tzedakah*, it is easy to respond, since the funds are always ready to be disbursed.

Our verse alludes to this course of action. ויקחו לי תרומה, *and let them take for Me an offering*, let them set aside their offerings, whenever they are in a giving mood; then it will be easy for the poor and the needy to collect. מאת כל איש אשר ידבנו לבו, *from every man whose heart makes him willing,* תקחו את תרומתי they shall take from the funds that have previously been designated as My offerings.

Chomas Anoch

Terumah

[כה:ב] דבר אל בני ישראל ויקחו לי תרומה מאת כל איש אשר ידבנו לבו תקחו את תרומתי.

[25:2] Speak to the people of Yisrael, and let them take for Me an offering; from every man whose heart makes him willing shall you take My offering.

ויקחו לי תרומה . . .
and let them take for Me an offering . . .

Tanna Dvei Eliyahu teaches that at the moment the people of Yisrael pronounced the words "We will do and we will heed," Hashem decided to give this high-minded concept tangible expression and said, "Let them take for Me an offering."

Based on this divine response, it has become customary that every person called to the Torah pledges a contribution to the synagogue or another charitable institution. He thereby expresses the concept that Torah, prayer and acts of kindness are the cornerstones of Judaism. This custom recalls *Mattan Torah*, the Giving of the Torah, when the people of Yisrael said, "We will do and we will heed," and Hashem replied, "Let them take for me an offering." The people of Yisrael complied in full measure, as it says in *Shemos* 36:5: "The people bring much more than necessary."

Rabbi Langner of Kinihanitch

ויקחו לי תרומה . . .
and let them take for Me an offering . . .

This verse ushers in the chapter of the building of the *Mishkan*, Sanctuary. After the completion of the detailed instructions to Moshe for the construction of the Sanctuary, the Torah goes on to mention the laws of *Shabbos (Shemos* 31:13-18). By contrast, when Moshe reviews these instructions with the people of Yisrael he prefaces them with a reference to *Shabbos* (35:1-3), reversing the order by placing *Shabbos* before the *Mishkan*.

This inversion may be understood if we recognize the respective connotations of the concepts of *Shabbos* and *Mishkan*. *Shabbos* implies the homage we pay to Hashem. By observing this day with rest and sanctity, we declare Hashem as the Creator of the Universe, Who ceased to work on the seventh day. *Mishkan* suggests the greatness of Yisrael. It is a testimony that Hashem singled out the people of Yisrael from among the nations and made His dwelling place among them.

Hashem placed the laws of the *Mishkan* before those of *Shabbos*, thereby demonstrating His preference of Yisrael's glory over His own. Moshe Rabbeinu, on the other hand, accorded priority to the *Shabbos* over the *Mishkan*, since from Moshe's perspective, Hashem's honor took precedence.

Kli Yakar

Author's note:

In a similar vein, the Rebbe of Barditchev explained the two names of *Pesach—Chag Hapesach*, the Festival of Passover, and *Chag Hamatzos*, the Festival of the Unleavened Bread. Yisrael called it *Chag Hapesach* in honor of Hashem, Who passed over our houses. Hashem called it *Chag Hamatzos* to glorify Yisrael who keep His commandment to eat the *matzos*.

and let them take for Me an offering . . . ויקחו לי תרומה . . .

Parshas Terumah, the portion of the Torah that details the offerings the people of Yisrael were to make, is preceded by *Parshas Mishpatim*, the portion that deals with civil and criminal law. There is a lesson in this for us all.

One is permitted to give to charity only if one is certain beyond a shadow of a doubt that the money he donates is truly his own and was earned justly and honestly, without breaking

[כה:ב] דבר אל בני ישראל ויקחו לי תרומה מאת כל איש אשר ידבנו לבו תקחו את תרומתי.

[25:2] Speak to the people of Yisrael, and let them take for Me an offering; from every man whose heart makes him willing shall you take My offering.

TORAH TREASURES • *Terumah*

any civil or criminal law.

Bais Halevi

A similar concept is expressed by the Chida: By rearranging the letters of the word תרומה, the word המותר emerges, which means "that which is permissible."

By equating תרומה and המותר we are saying, in effect, that *tzedakah* must be given from resources that were obtained legally, but not from ill-gotten means such as robbery or extortion, as it is written: "Establish me in justice and remove me from oppression."

Chomas Anoch

[כה:ב] דבר אל בני ישראל ויקחו לי תרומה מאת כל איש אשר ידבנו לבו תקחו את תרומתי.

[25:2] **Speak to the people of Yisrael, and let them take for Me an offering; from every man whose heart makes him willing shall you take My offering.**

... תקחו את תרומתי

... shall you take My offering

The verb תקחו, *you shall take*, is written in the second person plural, rather than תקח, the second person singular. This is in accordance with the rule that *tzedakah* must be collected by no fewer than two people.

A further indication for this rule is found in the numerical equivalence of תקחו, *you shall take*, and שנים יקחו, *let two people take*.

Baal Haturim

[כה:י] ועשו ארון עצי שטים אמתים וחצי ארכו ואמה וחצי רחבו ואמה וחצי קמתו.

[25:10] **And they shall make an ark of acacia wood, two cubits and a half shall be its length, a cubit and a half its breadth and a cubit and a half its height.**

... ועשו ארון עצי שטים אמתים וחצי ארכו

And they shall make an ark of acacia wood, two cubits and a half shall be its length ...

It is intriguing to note that the three dimensions of the ark are not whole numbers, but that they all contain a fraction of one half. These fractions of one half teach the fundamental lesson that a Torah scholar must be humble and contrite, constantly aware of having achieved only half of his objectives of perfection in Torah learning and devotion to Hashem.

Baal Haturim

ועשו ארון עצי שטים ...
And they shall make an ark of acacia wood ...

The basic theme of the Torah is teaching a Jew how to conduct his life. This concept is reflected in the fact that the entire *aleph bais* is contained within the verses describing the ark, the ark being the repository of the *Luchos*, the two Tablets of the Covenant. The only exception is the letter ג, *gimel*, the reason being that ג, *gimel*, recalls the word *gemul*, reward, and a person should not observe the Torah for the sake of receiving reward.

Nonetheless, there is abundant reward in store for those who fulfill Hashem's commands. This is expressed in the juxtaposition of the chapter of the ark and the chapter of the table, indicating the material rewards that will be bestowed even in *Olam Hazeh*, this world. The chapter of the table is followed by the verses concerning the *Menorah*, the candelabrum, as an allusion to the spiritual rewards awaiting the righteous in *Olam Habo*, the World to Come.

Otzar Chaim

אמתים וחצי ארכו ...
... two cubits and a half shall be its length

The *Gemara* in *Sanhedrin* 29a makes a somewhat cryptic comment on this verse.

The *Gemara* wants to know the source for the Rabbinic statement that "adding overmuch is tantamount to subtraction," and the *Gemara* finds the source in the abovemen-

[כה:י] ועשו ארון עצי שטים אמתים וחצי ארכו ואמה וחצי רחבו ואמה וחצי קמתו.

[25:10] And they shall make an ark of acacia wood, two cubits and a half shall be its length, a cubit and a half its breadth and a cubit and a half its height.

TORAH TREASURES • *Terumah*

tioned verse, "two cubits and a half shall be its length."

How does our verse prove this statement? Our verse states unequivocally that אמתים וחצי ארכו, *the length of the ark shall be two and a half cubits*. However, if we were to delete the letter ו, *vav*, from the word וחצי, the phrase would then read אמתים חצי ארכו, *"two cubits are half its length,"* resulting in a total length of four cubits, whereas its actual length was mandated to be two and one half cubits.

Thus, it becomes evident that with the addition of the letter ו, *vav*, to the word חצי, the length of the ark was reduced from four to two and one half cubits, proving that by adding you actually diminish.

Vilna Gaon

[כה:טו] בטבעת הארן יהיו הבדים לא יסרו ממנו.

[25:15] **The poles shall be in the rings of the ark; they shall not be removed from it.**

בטבעת הארן יהיו הבדים לא יסרו ממנו
The poles shall be in the rings of the ark; they shall not be removed from it

The Rambam suggests that the *Menorah* in the *Bais Hamikdash* was lit even during the daytime, since lighting the *Menorah* was an integral part of *Hatovas Haneros*, preparing the lights. The basis for this view is the Rabbinic statement that the *Menorah* was not needed for illumination. In order to demonstrate for all that the *Menorah* was not meant to be a source of light, the Torah commanded that it be kindled during the daytime, and the inference will thus be drawn that even at night it is not meant as a source of light.

The same reasoning applies in our verse.

The Torah commands that the poles remain in the rings of the ark, never to be removed, in order to indicate that they were not needed to transport the ark, since "the ark carries itself."

196

תרומה • TORAH TREASURES

(*Sotah* 35) Just as the poles in the rings were certainly not needed when the ark was at rest, neither were they needed when the ark was being moved, for "the ark carries itself."

Meshech Chochmah

בטבעת הארן יהיו הבדים לא יסרו ממנו
The poles shall be in the rings of the ark; they shall not be removed from it

The ark is unusual in that it is the only one of the furnishings of the Sanctuary whose poles are not to be removed.

Why is this so?

Since the ark is the repository of the Torah, the poles, in a sense, are the "bearers of the Torah," its supporters. Thus, our verse teaches us that the bearers of the Torah must be an integral part of it. A patron of Torah must be inseparable from it, attached to it, and he must adhere to its tenets.

Otzar Chaim

. . . מקשה תעשה אתם משני קצות הכפרת
. . . wrought from the two ends of the cover shall you make them

Rashi explains that they should not be made separately, fastening them to the ends of the cover after completing them. This divine command expresses allegorically a fundamental principle of child rearing.

The child-faced cherubim symbolically represent our children. The cherubim shall not be made individually and, upon completion, attached to the ark-cover. In other words, we must not raise our children with a culture and values alien to Torah and, after they have matured and absorbed this way of life, belat-

[כה:טו] בטבעת הארן יהיו הבדים לא יסרו ממנו.

[25:15] **The poles shall be in the rings of the ark; they shall not be removed from it.**

[כה:יח] ועשית שנים כרבים זהב מקשה תעשה אתם משני קצות הכפרת.

[25:18] **And you shall make two golden cherubim, wrought from the two ends of the cover shall you make them.**

TORAH TREASURES • *Terumah*

edly introduce them to Torah. The cherubim must be fashioned as an integral part of the cover. Our children must be educated in the pure and unadulterated spirit of the Torah.

Meir Eynei Yesharim

[כה:כ] והיו הכרבים פרשי כנפים למעלה סככים בכנפיהם על הכפרת ופניהם איש אל אחיו אל הכפרת יהיו פני הכרבים.

[25:20] **And the cherubim shall be made with wings spread upwards, screening the cover with their wings, and facing each other, toward the cover shall the faces of the cherubim be.**

...ופניהם איש אל אחיו
... and facing each other

The *Gemara* in *Bava Basra* finds a discrepancy between this verse, which states that the cherubim should be made "facing each other," and the verse in *Divrei Hayamim II* 3:13, which states that "their faces were turned toward the house." The *Gemara* reconciles this apparent contradiction by explaining that our verse refers to the time when the people of Yisrael act according to Hashem's Will, the other verse to a period when the people of Yisrael act contrary to His Will.

"And facing each other" refers to when "the people of Yisrael act according to Hashem's will," meaning that the Jews are also "facing each other"; they take an interest in their fellow Jew's welfare and treat him with brotherly love.

"With their faces toward the house" refers to when "the people of Yisrael act contrary to Hashem's Will," meaning that Jews face "toward the house," being concerned only with themselves, with the needs of their house; they turn a deaf ear to the suffering of others.

Indeed, the direction of the cherubim's faces, towards one another or towards the house, reflects the attitude of one Jew toward his fellow Jew.

Rabbi Yitzchak Elchanan Spector

תרומה • TORAH TREASURES

. . . ופניהם איש אל אחיו אל הכפרת יהיו פני הכרובים
. . . and facing each other, toward the cover shall the faces of the cherubim be

The *Talmud Yerushalmi* in the first chapter of *Shekalim* tells us that the gold of the ark-cover was an atonement for the sin of the golden calf. The question arises: Since we know from numerous *Talmudic* and *Midrashic* sources that *all* the gifts to the *Mishkan* atoned for the sin of the golden calf, why then does the *Yerushalmi* single out the ark-cover as the specific agent for atonement?

The ark-cover is unusual in that it is adorned with the cherubim which face each other, as well as the ark-cover. This arrangement symbolically represents Yisrael's attachment to Hashem, and as a result, the Divine Providence that shields Yisrael.

Yisrael's attachment to Hashem becomes manifest through the study of Hashem's Word as it is revealed in the Torah. To the degree that we engross ourselves in the Torah, Hashem's heavenly protection increases or diminishes.

This idea is represented in the cherubim whose faces are turned toward the ark-cover. This indicates that the bond with Hashem can only be established if the Jewish people direct their thoughts toward the ark, the repository of the Torah. There must be a complete acceptance of the dictates of Torah.

This affords us a new insight into the statement of the *Yerushalmi* that the gold of the ark-cover atoned for the sin of the golden calf.

The golden calf was the product of Yisrael's reliance on their own intellectual faculties. Their reasoning power induced them to construct something that was outside the realm of Torah. (When Yisrael noticed that Moshe

[כה:כ] והיו הכרבים פרשי כנפים למעלה סככים בכנפיהם על הכפרת ופניהם איש אל אחיו אל הכפרת יהיו פני הכרבים.

[25:20] And the cherubim shall be made with wings spread upwards, screening the cover with their wings, and facing each other, toward the cover shall the faces of the cherubim be.

TORAH TREASURES • *Terumah*

did not return from his heavenly sojourn, they wished to establish a special chamber that would be suited for communicating with Hashem. Even though their intentions were virtuous, their deeds were erroneous and resulted in a golden calf. Any act that is not grounded in Torah is useless. More than that, it is a sinful act.)

The gold of the ark-cover is the appropriate atonement for this sin, since it is a symbolic demonstration that Yisrael's attachment to Hashem is predicated on Torah alone.

Bais Halevi

[כה:כג] ועשית שלחן עצי שטים אמתים ארכו ואמה רחבו ואמה וחצי קמתו.

[25:23] **And you shall make a table of acacia wood, two cubits shall be its length, one cubit its width and a cubit and a half its height.**

ועשית שלחן . . .

And you shall make a table . . .

Why does the chapter describing the table immediately follow the chapter describing the ark?

This alludes to the *Mishnah* in *Avos* 3:4 that if two people eat at the same table and discuss Torah, it is as if they have eaten from the table of the Omnipresent.

Rabbeinu Efraim

[כה:לא] ועשית מנרת זהב טהור מקשה תיעשה המנורה ירכה וקנה גביעיה כפתריה ופרחיה ממנה יהיו.

[25:31] **And you shall make a candelabrum of pure gold, you shall make the candelabrum of wrought gold, it base, its shaft, its cups, its knobs and its flowers being of one piece with it.**

ועשית מנרת זהב טהור . . .

And you shall make a candelabrum of pure gold . . .

The *Midrash* opens its commentary on the Torah by quoting the verse from *Tehillim* (119:130): "The opening of Your Words gives light."

The Vilna Gaon explains this comment by focusing on the literal meaning of this passage in *Tehillim*.

"The opening of Your Words" means the words in the initial verse in each of the five

Books of the *Chumash*. "Gives light" means that these words allude to the *Menorah* that illuminated the Sanctuary.

The first verse of *Beraishis* has seven words, hinting at the seven arms of the menorah (the shaft and the six branches). The first verse of *Shemos* has eleven words, corresponding to the eleven knobs. The first verse of *Vayikra* has nine words, alluding to the nine flowers. The first verse of *Bamidbar* (including the unit 1) has eighteen words, corresponding to the height of the *Menorah* which was 18 handbreadths. The first verse of *Devarim* has twenty two words, corresponding to the twenty two cups.

Divrei Eliyahu

[כה:לא] **ועשית מנרת**
זהב טהור מקשה תיעשה
המנורה ירכה וקנה
גביעיה כפתריה ופרחיה
ממנה יהיו.

[25:31] **And you shall make a candelabrum of pure gold, you shall make the candelabrum of wrought gold, it base, its shaft, its cups, its knobs and its flowers being of one piece with it.**

Tetzaveh / תצוה

ואתה תצוה ...
And you shall instruct ...

The name of Moshe Rabbeinu does not appear anywhere in the portion of *Tetzaveh*. This is curious, since beginning with the chapter of his birth, the name Moshe appears in every subsequent *Parshah*.

The omission of Moshe's name from *Parshas Tetzaveh* represents Hashem's compliance with his request (*Shemos* 32:32): "And now, please forgive their sin, and if not, please blot me out of Your book that You have written."

The *Gemara* (*Makkos* 11a) states that a curse uttered by a righteous person, even a conditional curse, will come to pass. This was its fulfillment.

But why in the portion of *Tetzaveh*?

Moshe, with supreme selflessness, stayed Hashem's wrath against Yisrael. In his honor, the portion of *Tetzaveh* was chosen as the one from which his name was blotted out, for *Tetzaveh* is essentially a continuation of the story of the construction of the *Mishkan* that began

[כז:כ] ואתה תצוה את בני ישראל ויקחו אליך שמן זית זך כתית למאור להעלת נר תמיד.

[27:20] **And you shall instruct the people of Yisrael that they bring to you pure olive oil, pressed and prepared for giving light, to light up a perpetual lamp.**

TORAH TREASURES • *Tetzaveh*

in the portion of *Terumah*, and as such it is actually part and parcel of *Terumah*. Since in *Terumah* the name Moshe is mentioned several times, it can be said that, in a sense, his name is not missing from any portion in the Torah.

Continuing this trend of thought, the *Zohar* states that the Torah is divided into 53 weekly portions. However, the Maharam notes that there are 54 portions.

The R'ash Abohav reconciles the discrepancy by observing that the portion *Vezos Haberachah*, which is read on *Simchas Torah*, is generally read on a weekday. In this respect, it differs from the other portions which are all read on *Shabbos*. Because of this, the *Zohar* does not include it in the count. However, predicated on the premise that *Tetzaveh* can be considered an integral part of *Terumah*, it may be said that the reason for the *Zohar's* total of 53 Torah portions is that *Terumah* and *Tetzaveh* are counted as one.

Chomas Anoch

[כז:כ] ואתה תצוה את בני ישראל ויקחו אליך שמן זית זך כתית למאור להעלות נר תמיד.

[27:20] **And you shall instruct the people of Yisrael that they bring to you pure olive oil, pressed and prepared for giving light, to light up a perpetual lamp.**

ואתה תצוה את בני ישראל . . .
And you shall instruct the people of Yisrael . . .

The fact that Moshe Rabbeinu's name is not mentioned in this weekly portion is attributable to his prayer to Hashem (*Shemos* 32:32): "And now, please forgive their sin, and if not, please blot me out of Your book that You have written."

Why, of all portions, was his name eliminated from *Tetzaveh*? It is because the anniversary of Moshe's death, the 7th of *Adar*, always occurs during the week in which this portion is read, and death symbolizes departure or elimination.

Nevertheless, the name Moshe does appear in *Tetzaveh*, albeit in a concealed form. We must preface this exposition with a brief explanation.

Every letter of the *aleph bais* consists of a revealed and a concealed part. For instance, the letter ב, *bais*, is written בית, the ב being the revealed part and the י, *yud*, and ת, *tuf*, being the concealed part.

Now we can understand the exposition. The portion of *Tetzaveh* contains 101 verses. Similarly, the sum total of the concealed parts of the letters משה, *Moshe*, is also 101. מ, *mem*, is spelled out as מם, ם being the concealed part with a numerical value of 40; ש, *shin*, is spelled out as שין, ין being the concealed part with a numerical value of 60; ה, *heh*, is spelled out as הא, א being the concealed part with a numerical value of 1. The total is 101, the exact number of verses in the portion of *Tetzaveh*.

Vilna Gaon

ואתה תצוה את בני ישראל . . .
And you shall instruct the people of Yisrael . . .

Rabbeinu Ephraim notes that Moshe was originally destined to become the *Kohein Gadol*, the High Priest. However, when Moshe refused to fulfill Hashem's mission (*Shemos* 4:13) and Aharon became the appointed spokesman, Moshe forfeited the priesthood and Aharon was ordained *Kohein Gadol* instead. Since the portion of *Tetzaveh* describes the priestly vestments and the investiture of Aharon and his sons as priests, the name of Moshe is not mentioned.

The inescapable conclusion to be drawn from Rabbeinu Ephraim's statement is that the omission of Moshe's name from *Tetzaveh* is

[כז:כ] ואתה תצוה את בני ישראל ויקחו אליך שמן זית זך כתית למאור להעלת נר תמיד.

[27:20] **And you shall instruct the people of Yisrael that they bring to you pure olive oil, pressed and prepared for giving light, to light up a perpetual lamp.**

to be construed as a rebuke to Moshe for having caused the priesthood to be transferred to Aharon.

Nachal Kedumim

... ויקחו אליך שמן זית זך כתית למאור
... that they bring to you pure olive oil, pressed and prepared for giving light

The numerical value of the word כתית, *pressed*, amounts to 830. The first *Bais Hamikdash* remained standing for 410 years; the second *Bais Hamikdash*, endured 420 years. Thus, 830 represents the entire length of time the *Bais Hamikdash* existed, during which the *Menorah* in the Sanctuary was lit.

Baal Haturim

[כח:ח] וחשב אפדתו אשר עליו כמעשהו ממנו יהיה זהב תכלת וארגמן ותולעת שני ושש משזר.

[28:8] And the skillfully woven band which is upon it shall be made in the same way and of one piece with it, of gold thread, blue, indigo and scarlet wool and fine twined linen.

... וחשב אפדתו אשר עליו כמעשהו ממנו יהיה
And the skillfully woven band which is upon it shall be made in the same way and of one piece with it ...

Homiletically translated, this passage yields a profound thought on Torah ethics.

וחשב from the verb חשב, *to think*, is translated as the thought or intention, and אפדתו from אפוד, *to adorn or dress up*. Thus, וחשב אפדתו becomes *the thought of preparing oneself for the performance of a mitzvah.* כמעשהו ממנו יהיה, *the thought itself is regarded as the actual deed.*

In other words, the intention to do a *mitzvah* is rewarded by Hashem as though the *mitzvah* had in fact already been performed.

Rabbeinu Efraim

תצוה • TORAH TREASURES

וחשב אפדתו אשר עליו כמעשהו ממנו יהיה . . .
And the skillfully woven band which is upon it shall be made in the same way and of one piece with it . . .

Our Sages teach that through the *ephod*, atonement was granted for the sin of idolatry. This sin is regarded with such severity that the intent to commit idolatry is judged as harshly as the sinful act itself. Our verse alludes to this.

וחשב, *the mere thought or intent to commit*, אפדתו, *the sin for which the ephod offers atonement, i.e. idolatry*, כמעשהו, *is judged as severely as the act of idolatry itself.*

Nachal Kedumim

. . . ונשמע קולו בבאו אל הקדש
. . . and the sound (of the bells) shall be heard when he goes into the holy place

The *Massorah* perceives a close relationship between the abovementioned verse and two other verses in which the word ונשמע, *and we will listen or heed*, appears. One is in *Shemos* 24:7: נעשה ונשמע, "*We will do and we will heed.*" The other is in *Megillas Esther* 1:20: ונשמע פתגם המלך אשר יעשה, "*And the king's decree shall be heard.*"

The common thread running through these three passages may be found in the *Gemara* (*Megillah* 3b): Rabah states that as the reading of the *Megillah* takes precedence over the study of Torah, so does the reading of the *Megillah* take precedence over the *avodah*, the service in the *Bais Hamikdash*.

The three verses cited by the *Massorah* correspond to the three concepts mentioned by Rabah: Torah study, the service in the *Bais*

[כח:לה] והיה על אהרן לשרת ונשמע קולו בבאו אל הקדש לפני ה' ובצאתו ולא ימות.

[28:35] **And Aharon shall wear it when he performs the service, and the sound (of the bells) shall be heard when he goes into the holy place before Hashem, and when he comes out, so that he will not die.**

207

TORAH TREASURES • *Tetzaveh*

Hamikdash and the reading of the *Megillah*. נעשה ונשמע, *we will do and we will heed*, alludes to Torah study. ונשמע קולו בבאו אל הקדש, *and the sound (of the bells) shall be heard when he goes into the holy place*, refers to the service in the *Bais Hamikdash*. ונשמע פתגם המלך אשר יעשה, *and the king's decree shall be heard*, alludes to the reading of the *Megillah*.

This last phrase is followed in the text by the words כי רבה היא, *for it is great*, thus indicating that the reading of the *Megillah* is of overriding importance and takes precedence over the other two concepts, namely Torah study and the service in the *Bais Hamikdash*.

Otzar Chaim

[כח:לה] והיה על אהרן לשרת ונשמע קולו בבאו אל הקדש לפני ה' ובצאתו ולא ימות.

[28:35] And Aharon shall wear it when he performs the service, and the sound (of the bells) shall be heard when he goes into the holy place before Hashem, and when he comes out, so that he will not die.

. . . ונשמע קולו בבאו אל הקדש
. . . and the sound (of the bells) shall be heard when he goes into the holy place

This verse can be taken as an admonition directed at the leaders of the Jewish nation.

Sometimes these men are by nature reserved and reticent, reluctant to raise their voice. Humility, to be sure, is an admirable trait but only in everyday matters. However, when confronted with the desecration of Hashem's Holy Name, when the sanctity of Torah is under attack, they must speak out forcefully in defense of all that is holy.

As our verse states: "Let his voice be heard when he goes into the holy place." When Torah is under siege, it is time to join in relentless battle against those who defame Hashem's Word.

Chasam Sofer

תצוה • TORAH TREASURES

... ופתחת עליו פתוחי חתם קדש לה'
... and engrave upon it like the engravings of a signet: Holy to Hashem

The *Gemara* (*Ta'anis* 2a) tells us that there are three keys which were not entrusted to a heavenly messenger but remain under the control of Hashem: the key to the birth process, the key to the resurrection of the dead and the key to rain.

Our verse hints at these with the words פתוחי חתם קדש לה', *the engravings of a signet: Holy to Hashem.* פתוחי is derived from the verb פתח, *to open,* hence the key which unlocks the door to חתם, an acronym formed by the initial letters of the three fundamentals mentioned in the *Gemara*: ח, *ches,* for חיה, *a mother in childbed,* ת, *tuf,* for תחית המתים, *resurrection of the dead,* and מ, *mem,* for מטר, *rain.* The verse concludes, 'קדש לה, *these three are holy and consecrated to Hashem*; they are not delivered into the hands of a messenger.

Vilna Gaon

[כח:לו] ועשית ציץ זהב טהור ופתחת עליו פתוחי חתם קדש לה'.

[28:36] And you shall make a plate of pure gold and engrave upon it like the engravings of a signet: Holy to Hashem.

Ki Sissa / כי תשא

כי תשא את ראש בני ישראל ...
When you take a head count of the people of Yisrael ...

In the weekly portion of *Ki Sissa*, the first two segments (*Kohein* and *Levi*) are uncharacteristically lengthy. In fact, the better part of the entire portion is apportioned to them. This uneven division is in keeping with the statement in the *Gemara* (*Bava Metzia* 59b) that one should not say "Please hang up this fish for me" to someone whose relative was executed by hanging; any reference to hanging might easily be misconstrued as a hint at "the skeleton in the family closet."

The first two segments of *Ki Sissa* contain the narration of the *chet ha'egel*, the sin of the golden calf. Therefore, we call up a *Kohein* and a *Levi* for the entire reading of this story, because their ancestors, the tribe of Levi, did not take part in its nefarious worship, and they will not be offended by it.

Rabbi Meir of Ostrowtza

[ל:יב] כי תשא את ראש בני ישראל לפקדיהם ונתנו איש כפר נפשו לה' בפקד אתם ולא יהיה בהם נגף בפקד אתם.

[30:12] When you take a head count of the people of Yisrael to establish their numbers, then they shall each give compensation for his soul to Hashem whereby to be counted, so that there be no plague among them when they are counted.

‎. . . ונתנו איש כפר נפשו
. . . then they shall each give compensation for his soul

The word ונתנו, *then they shall give*, is what is known as a palindrome, a word that reads the same backward as forward. This unusual feature is a hint that one who gives today may someday be on the receiving side himself.

This idea is expressed by the two cantillation signs on the word ונתנו, namely *kadma ve'azla*, which literally translates to "comes first" and "goes away." Truly, wealth is like a revolving wheel, it comes and it goes. This conforms to the rabbinic statement: "Be the first to offer bread to the poor, in order that others may someday offer bread to your children."

Vilna Gaon

Author's Note:
Baal Haturim offers a somewhat different interpretation. Noting that ונתנו reads the same backward as forward, he explains: "Whatever anyone gives to charity will be returned to him, his fortune will never be diminished because of the charity he gave."

[יג: ל] זה יתנו כל העבר על הפקדים מחצית השקל בשקל הקדש עשרים גרה השקל מחצית השקל תרומה לה'.

[30:13] **This they shall give, every one that passes to be counted, half a shekel according to the shekel of the sanctuary, each shekel being twenty gerah, half a shekel being the offering to Hashem.**

. . . מחצית השקל
. . . half a shekel

If we scrutinize the word מחצית, *half*, we note that the two letters closest to the צ, *tzadi*, are ח, *ches*, and י, *yud*, which together spell חי, *life*, the two other letters, those distant from the *tzadi*, are מ, *mem*, and ת, *suf*, which together spell מת, *dead*.

This order of the letters suggests that a person closely attached to the *mitzvah* of *tzedakah* (the letter *tzadi* symbolizing *tzedakah*, charity) will merit long life, but one distant from this *mitzvah* places his life in jeopardy, as it is indeed written, "But charity delivers from death." (*Mishlei* 10:2)

Rabbi Aaron of Karlin

‏. . . מבן עשרים שנה ומעלה
... from twenty years old and upward

The last letters of the words ‏מבן עשרים שנה, *from twenty years old*, when placed in reverse order, form the acronym ‏המן, *Haman*.

Haman offered to pay ten thousand talents of silver to King Achashverosh for the right to destroy the Jewish people (*Esther* 3:9). Finding his name concealed in the chapter that discusses the giving of *shekalim*, indicates in a veiled manner that the Jewish *shekalim* would be triumphant over those that Haman gave. This concept is clearly spelled out in the *Gemara* (*Megillah* 13b).

Baal Haturim

[30:14] Everyone that passes to be counted, from twenty years old and upward, shall give the offering of Hashem.

‏. . . העשיר לא ירבה
The rich man shall not give more ...

The cantillation signs on the words ‏העשיר לא ירבה, *the rich man shall not give more*, are called *munach revi'i*, which literally translates to "leave four." These signs bring to mind the *Gemara* in *Kesuvos* 50a which states, relating to the giving of charity, that one should not give away more than one fifth of his fortune. This concept is implied by the cantillation signs. In other words, "the rich man shall not give more" than one fifth share of a share of his income, so that for each share he donates, he leaves four shares for himself, *munach revi'i*.

Vilna Gaon

[30:15] The rich man shall not give more and the poor man shall not give less than the half shekel when they give the offering to Hashem to atone for your souls.

TORAH TREASURES • *Ki Sissa*

[כג: ל] ואתה קח לך בשמים ראש מר דרור חמש מאות וקנמן בשם מחציתו חמשים ומאתים וקנה בשם חמשים ומאתים.

[30:23] **Take for yourself the finest spices, flowing myrrh for five hundred shekels, fragrant cinnamon in halves, each for two hundred and fifty, and fragrant stalks for two hundred and fifty.**

קח לך בשמים ...
Take for yourself the finest spices ...

The last letters of the words קח לך בשמים, *take for yourself the finest spices*, form the acronym חכם, *a wise man*, the implication being that there exists a relationship between fragrance and wisdom. Indeed, we find such a connection in the *Gemara* (*Yoma* 76b) which states that wine and spices are conducive to wisdom, for they gratify and soothe man's spirit and free his mind for unencumbered thought.

Rabbeinu Efraim

... מר דרור
... flowing myrrh

The *Gemara* in *Chullin* wants to know where we find an allusion to מרדכי, *Mordechai*, in the Torah, and the *Gemara* answers that it is in the words מר דרור, *flowing myrrh*.

It is obvious that there is more to this allusion than the apparent resemblance of the words מר דרור and מרדכי.

A closer inspection of the words מר דרור reveals that מר has the same numerical value as עמלק, *Amalek*, of whom Haman was a descendant.

Furthermore, the *gematria* of דרור equals that of הוא חפשי, *he is free*. (Actually, the word דרור itself also means freedom.) A more profound relationship between מרדכי and מר דרור is suggested by this *gematria*. It is as if to say that even when confronted with the overpowering might of מר, an allusion to Amalek, הוא חפשי, *he (Mordechai) remains free and independent*. Amalek will never be able to defeat him, as it is written, "But Mordechai did not bow down or prostrate himself before him." (*Esther* 3:2) Mordechai the Jew remains forever

indomitable in body and spirit.
Traditional

... משחת קדש
... a holy anointing oil

The phrase משחת קדש, *a holy anointing oil*, is mentioned three times in the weekly portion of *Ki Sissa*, twice in this verse and once in verse 30:31: "And you shall speak to the people of Yisrael saying: 'This shall be a holy anointing oil to Me throughout your generations.' "

This threefold mention of holy anointing oil foreshadows the three kings of Yisrael who were anointed with *shemen hamishchah*, holy anointing oil: Shaul, David and Shlomo.

Mahari of Worms

Author's Note:
According to the commentators Redak, Abarbanel and *Kli Yakar*, Shaul was not anointed with *shemen hamishchah*. *Pirkei d'Rabbi Eliezer* and *Midrash Rabba*, however, corroborate Mahari's view that Shaul was indeed anointed with *shemen hamishchah*. Rashi and Rambam concur with the latter.

[ל:כה] ועשית אתו שמן משחת קדש רקח מרקחת מעשה רקח שמן משחת קדש יהיה.

[30:25] **And you shall make it a holy anointing oil, a perfume compounded according to the art of the perfumer; it shall be a holy anointing oil.**

... בצלאל בן אורי בן חור
Bezalel, the son of Uri, the son of Chur ...

The question arises: Why is Bezalel's lineage traced to his grandfather, instead of the simpler and more common "Bezalel the son of Uri"?

The answer lies in the fact that the *Mishkan*, the Tabernacle, was an atonement for the worship of the Golden Calf. It should also be recalled that Chur, Bezalel's grandfather, died a martyr's death while opposing this act

[לא:ב] ראה קראתי בשם בצלאל בן אורי בן חור למטה יהודה.

[31:2] **See, I have called upon Bezalel, the son of Uri, the son of Chur, of the tribe of Yehudah.**

TORAH TREASURES • *Ki Sissa*

of idolatry. Therefore, for his courageous act, Chur merited that his grandson Bezalel, by building the *Mishkan*, would be instrumental in bringing about the atonement for the very sin which caused his grandfather's death. Since Bezalel was chosen by virtue of his grandfather, it is understandable that his lineage is traced to this grandfather.

Traditional

[לא:יד] ושמרתם את השבת כי קדש הוא לכם מחלליה מות יומת כי כל העשה בה מלאכה ונכרתה הנפש ההיא מקרב עמיה.

[31:14] **You shall observe the Sabbath for it is holy to you, those who desecrate it shall surely be put to death, for whoever does any work on it, then that soul shall be cut off from among its people.**

ושמרתם את השבת כי קדש הוא לכם מחלליה מות יומת . . .
You shall observe the Sabbath for it is holy to you, those who desecrate it shall surely be put to death . . .

The *Yerushalmi* relates that Rabbi Chiya visited a certain town where he observed someone cutting herbs on *Shabbos*. The next day he wrote him a note quoting the above-mentioned verse that "those who desecrate it shall surely be put to death."

The question arises: Why did Rabbi Chiya wait until the following day to write the note, rather than telling him the verse on the spot?

The answer can be deduced from the *Gemara* (*Megillah* 24b): Rabbi Chiya said to Rabbi Shimon b'Rebbi: "If you were a *Levi* you would not be qualified to sing in the *Bais Hamikdash* because your voice is too thick." He went and told this to his father, and his father said to him: "Go ask Rabbi Chiya if when he comes to the verse 'וחכיתי לה, *And I will wait for Hashem,* (*Yeshayah* 8:17) if he will not be a reviler and a blasphemer."

Rashi explains that because Rabbi Chiya pronounced the letter ח, *ches,* as ה, *hei,* he would articulate the words וחכיתי as והכיתי thereby changing the meaning of the verse to "and I will strike." Such an erroneous reading would be blasphemous indeed.

This being so, if Rabbi Chiya would have told the man מחלליה מות יומת, he would have enunciated it as מהלליה מות יומת, *"everyone that praises it shall surely be put to death,"* which is the opposite of the true meaning. He therefore sent the message in writing.

Vilna Gaon

ושמרו בני ישראל ...
And the people of Yisrael shall keep ...

[31:16] And the people of Yisrael shall keep the Sabbath, to establish the Sabbath for future generations as a perpetual covenant.

The word ושמרו in the context of this verse should be translated as "to look forward to, to anticipate eagerly," similar to Rashi's interpretation of שמר in the verse (*Beraishis* 37:11): "His father was looking forward to the day when Yosef's dreams would be fulfilled."

Accordingly, our text should be seen as a command not to perceive the *Shabbos* as a day of cumbersome restrictions and hindrances, but to look forward to its coming in eager anticipation as a day of joy and holiness.

Or Hachaim

... ויקרא אהרן ויאמר חג לה' מחר
... and Aharon called out and said: "Tomorrow shall be a festival to Hashem."

[32:5] And when Aharon saw this, he built an altar before it, and Aharon called out and said: "Tomorrow shall be a festival to Hashem."

Aharon's conduct at first glance appears incomprehensible.

Our Sages explain that his intentions in building the altar were meritorious, that he wished thereby to divert Hashem's wrath from the people to himself, and that he intended to delay the worship of the golden calf by impeding the construction of the altar. But what did Aharon mean when he declared, "Tomorrow shall be a festival to Hashem"?

For an answer, let us remember that the golden calf was produced on the 17th of *Tammuz*, on the same day Moshe shattered the *Luchos*, the Tablets of the Law, and that there will come a day when Hashem will turn this tragic day into a festival. In the words of the prophet (*Zechariah* 8:19): "Thus says Hashem of Hosts: 'The fast of the fourth month (i.e. the 17th of *Tammuz*) ... shall be for the House of Yehudah joy and gladness and cheerful festivals.'"

Thus, when Aharon proclaimed, "Tomorrow shall be a festival to Hashem," he was speaking metaphorically of a "tomorrow" in the distant future.

Nachal Kedumim

[לב:ח] סרו מהר מן הדרך אשר צויתם עשו להם עגל מסכה ...
They have been quick to abandon the way I instructed them to follow, they have made for themselves a molten calf-idol ...

The wording and syntax of this verse are rather peculiar and require an explanation.

Let us consider a hypothetical situation in which a person has the desire, Heaven forbid, to violate all the commandments of the Torah. Certainly, in order to achieve his "ambition", he will require a long time. He has to wait for *Pesach* before he can commit the sin of eating *chametz* and for *Yom Kippur* before he can transgress the command to fast, and so on. It would take a long time indeed to violate all 613 commandments.

But by worshipping idols he can achieve his aim instantly, for "idolatry is tantamount to a repudiation of the entire Torah."

This thought affords us a better insight into the meaning of the abovementioned verse.

[32:8] **They have been quick to abandon the way I instructed them to follow, they have made for themselves a molten calf-idol, and they have bowed down to it and sacrificed to it and said: "This is your lord, O Yisrael, which brought you up out of the land of Egypt."**

"They have been quick to abandon the way I instructed them to follow, they have made for themselves a molten calf-idol." By committing idolatry they have accomplished this instantaneously.

Nachal Kedumim

... ולכלתם מעל פני האדמה
... and to wipe them off the face of the earth

The last letters of these words, ולכלתם מעל פני האדמה, *and to wipe them off the face of the earth*, if rearranged, yield the word מילה, *circumcision*. This simple acronym contains the very essence of Moshe's appeal to Hashem for clemency for the people of Yisrael.

Moshe's argument was predicated on the fact, mentioned in the *Midrash*, that Pharaoh had warned, "I see in my astrological signs that a constellation named *Ra'ah* is in ascendancy. It will reach its zenith when you will be in the Desert. This is an ominous sign, a portent of blood and killing."

After the *chet ha'egel*, the sin of the golden calf, when Hashem threatened to annihilate Israel, Moshe pleaded that the Egyptians would say: "For evil (under the star *Ra'ah*) did He bring them forth, to kill them in the mountains and to wipe them off the face of the earth." In other words, Moshe was arguing that if Hashem destroyed Yisrael, Pharaoh's prediction would come true. Thereupon, Hashem immediately acceded to Moshe's prayers and transformed the blood that was predestined for them from "blood of slaughter" to "blood of circumcision." For upon entering Eretz Yisrael, Yehoshua circumcised them, since they could not be circumcised in the desert.

Ohel Yitzchak

[לב:יב] למה יאמרו מצרים לאמר ברעה הוציאם להרג אתם בהרים ולכלתם מעל פני האדמה שוב מחרון אפך והנחם על הרעה לעמך.

[32:12] Why should the Egyptians speak, saying: "For evil did He bring them forth, to kill them in the mountains and to wipe them off the face of the earth"? Turn back from Your fierce wrath and retract this evil against Your people.

TORAH TREASURES • *Ki Sissa*

[לג:כג] **והסרתי את כפי וראית את אחרי ופני לא יראו.**

[33:23] And I will take away My Hand, and you shall see My Back; but My Face shall not be seen.

... וראית את אחרי ופני לא יראו
... and you shall see My Back; but My Face shall not be seen

This verse, of course, must be understood in an anthropomorphic sense, in which human forms are attributed to Hashem. Figuratively, this passage expresses man's perception of Hashem's guiding Hand in world affairs. For such are the ways of Hashem. "You shall see My Back." Only long after an event has taken place do we grasp the divine justice manifest in it. "But My Face shall not be seen." At the time the event occurs, we cannot fathom the reason for Hashem's actions.

Chasam Sofer

[לד:יז-יח] **אלהי מסכה לא תעשה לך. את חג המצות תשמר שבעת ימים תאכל מצות אשר צויתך למועד חדש האביב כי בחדש האביב יצאת ממצרים.**

[34:17-18] You shall not make molten idols for yourself. You shall observe the Festival of Unleavened Bread, seven days shall you eat unleavened bread, as I commanded you at the time appointed in the month of early spring, for in the month of early spring did you go forth from Egypt.

... אלהי מסכה לא תעשה לך. את חג המצות תשמר
You shall not make molten idols for yourself. You shall observe the Festival of Unleavened Bread ...

For an understanding of the connection between these seemingly unrelated verses, let us turn to the *Gemara* (*Megillah* 12a) which asks why the Jews of the generation of Mordechai and Esther deserved to perish. The *Gemara* answers that it was because they bowed down to the idols of Nevuchadnezzar. The *Gemara* (*Megillah* 15a) also tells us that Mordechai found it necessary to fast on the first day of *Pesach*, thereby violating the joy of the festival of *Pesach*.

Based on these statements of the *Gemara*, the following connection can be established between our verses. "You shall not make molten idols for yourself." If you obey this law, you will not have to desecrate *Pesach* by fasting, as the Jews in the days of Mordechai and Esther had to do.

She'airis Yaakov

כי תשא • TORAH TREASURES

... ומשה לא ידע כי קרן עור פניו בדברו אתו
... and Moshe did not know that the skin of his face had become luminous when He had spoken with him

The *Midrash* teaches us that when the writing of the Torah was completed, there remained on the pen one drop of ink the size of the letter י, *yud*. Hashem placed this drop on Moshe's head, which caused it to send forth beams.

This theme is expressed in the phrase כי קרן עור פניו, *that the skin of his face had become luminous*, whereby כי should be read as כיוד, *as a yud*, a quantity of ink as small as a *yud*, had caused the glorious radiance of Moshe's face.

This *Midrash* prompted the following question by the *gaon* Rabbi Heschel. An imperfect person has to estimate the amount of ink he will need; as a result, he might have a surplus. By contrast, Hashem, being omniscient, certainly knew the precise quantity He would require and should not have had any leftover ink.

He explains, that when Moshe was to write the words והאיש משה ענו מאד, *And the man Moshe was very humble*, (Bamidbar 12:3) he was commanded to write the word עניו, *humble*, with a י, *yud*. Moshe, however, wrote in ענו, without a *yud*, as if to indicate that his humility was incomplete and lacking, which was in itself an expression of his great humility.

It was this letter *yud*, the letter that Moshe omitted from the word ענו, that was leftover. Hashem placed it on Moshe's face, which brought about its emanation of radiant luminescence.

Nachal Kedumim

[לד:כט] **ויהי ברדת משה מהר סיני ושני לחת העדת ביד משה ברדתו מן ההר ומשה לא ידע כי קרן עור פניו בדברו אתו.**

[34:29] And it happened when Moshe descended from Mount Sinai that the two Tablets of the Testimony were in Moshe's hand when he came down from the mount, and Moshe did not know that the skin of his face had become luminous when He had spoken with him.

TORAH TREASURES • *Ki Sissa*

[לד:כט] ויהי ברדת משה
מהר סיני ושני לחת
העדת ביד משה ברדתו
מן ההר ומשה לא ידע כי
קרן עור פניו בדברו אתו.

[34:29] And it happened when Moshe descended from Mount Sinai that the two Tablets of the Testimony were in Moshe's hand when he came down from the mount, and Moshe did not know that the skin of his face had become luminous when He had spoken with him.

Author's Note:

Rabbeinu Efraim finds an allusion to this *Midrash* in the verse (*Chavakuk* 3:4): קרנים מידו לו, *"He received radiance through His Hand."* The letters מידו, *through His Hand*, can be rearranged to read מדיו, *through ink*, altering the meaning of the verse to "he received radiance through ink."

An alternate rearrangement of מידו yields מיוד, through the letter *yud*, with the resulting translation "he received radiance from the letter *yud*."

Vayakheil / ויקהל

ויקהל משה ...

And Moshe assembled ...

Why did Moshe find it necessary to assemble the entire congregation of Yisrael for the proclamation of the building of the *Mishkan*? A possible answer may be found in the fact that the portion of *Vayakheil* deals with the *Mishkan*, which atoned for the *chet ha'egel*, the sin of the golden calf.

When the Torah narrates this sad chapter of national downfall, the story is introduced with the following verse (*Shemos* 32:1): "And the people saw that Moshe was taking too long to come down from the mountain, and the people assembled around Aharon, and they said to him: 'Arise and make us a deity to lead us ...'". Significantly, both in our verse and in the story of the golden calf, the Torah uses the term *vayakheil*, which denotes assembly, as if to say, "Let the *vayakheil* of the *Mishkan* be an atonement for the *vayakheil* of the *chet ha'egel*, the sin of the golden calf."

Otzar Chaim

[לה:א] ויקהל משה את כל עדת בני ישראל ויאמר אלהם אלא הדברים אשר צוה ה' לעשת אתם.

[35:1] **And Moshe assembled** all the congregation of the people of Yisrael and said to them: "These are the things which Hashem has commanded you to do."

TORAH TREASURES • *Vayakheil*

[לה:א] ויקהל משה את
כל עדת בני ישראל ויאמר
אלהם אלה הדברים אשר
צוה ה' לעשת אתם.

[35:1] **And Moshe assembled all the congregation of the people of Yisrael and said to them: "These are the things which Hashem has commanded you to do."**

ויקהל משה . . .

And Moshe assembled . . .

Why did Moshe find it necessary to assemble the entire congregation of Yisrael for the proclamation of the building of the *Mishkan*?

We read in *Shemos* 19:2 that at the time of *Mattan Torah*, the Giving of the Torah: ויחן שם ישראל נגד ההר, *"And Yisrael encamped there before the mountain."* The verb ויחן, *he encamped*, appears in the singular form rather than the plural ויחנו, *they encamped*.

This singular form is indicative of the strong feelings of unity that prevailed among them at that moment of transcendent holiness and purity. At the time of the *chet ha'egel*, the sin of the golden calf, this unity gave way to conflict, divisiveness and quarreling factions.

The portion of *Vayakheil* discusses the building of the *Mishkan*, the Tabernacle, which was erected as an atonement for the sin of the golden calf.

Therefore, before teaching the people of Yisrael the laws of the *Mishkan*, Moshe wanted to reestablish the peace and unity of purpose that had inspired them at the time of the Giving of the Torah. Hence, Moshe "assembled" and unified the entire congregation of Israel.

Eretz Chemdah

ויקהל משה . . .

And Moshe assembled . . .

Why did Moshe find it necessary to assemble the entire congregation of Yisrael for the proclamation of the building of the *Mishkan*?

Moshe saw through prophecy that the *Bais Hamikdash* would one day be destroyed through *sin'as chinam*, unwarranted hatred. Therefore, he wanted to strengthen the bonds of brotherhood and sympathy among the people of Yisrael before the building of the *Mishkan*, since this was a prerequisite for its endurance.

This prompted him to announce the laws concerning the tabernacle in the presence of "all the congregation of the people of Yisrael," in order to emphasize the importance of unity, peace and mutual understanding.

Al Hatorah

ויקהל משה . . . לא תבערו אש בכל משבתיכם ביום השבת
And Moshe assembled . . . You shall kindle no fire in any of your dwellings on the Sabbath day

The juxtaposition of the two verses "Moshe assembled" and "You shall kindle no fire" requires clarification.

The *Akeidas Yitzchak* explains it by metaphorically rendering "You shall kindle no fire . . ." as "You shall not kindle the fires of strife and dissension on the Sabbath day."

The prospects for discord are greater on *Shabbos*, for on that day people have the opportunity to pass the time with idle talk and gossip, which often brings bickering in its wake.

This explains the motive for Moshe's prefacing the laws of Shabbos with "Moshe assembled." Moshe tells the people of Yisrael that if they will spend the *Shabbos* in idle chatter there is an ever present danger of "kindling the fires of quarreling." To prevent this from happening, Moshe caused the people of Yisrael to assemble in unity, to spend the *Shabbos* together with their families in the learning of Torah and the pursuit of spiritual elevation.

Kli Yakar

[לה: א-ג] ויקהל משה את כל עדת בני ישראל ויאמר אלהם אלה הדברים אשר צוה ה' לעשת אתם. ששת ימים תעשה מלאכה וביום השביעי יהיה לכם קדש שבת שבתון לה' כל העשה בו מלאכה יומת. לא תבערו אש בכל משבתיכם ביום השבת

[35:1-3] And Moshe assembled all the congregation of the people of Yisrael and said to them: "These are the things which Hashem has commanded you to do." You shall do work for six days, but the seventh day shall be a holy day for you, a Sabbath day of rest to Hashem, whoever does any work on it shall be put to death. You shall kindle no fire in any of your dwellings on the Sabbath day.

TORAH TREASURES • *Vayakheil*

[לה:ב] ששת ימים תעשה מלאכה וביום השביעי יהיה לכם קדש שבת שבתון לה' כל העשה בו מלאכה יומת.

[35:2] **You shall do work for six days, but the seventh day shall be a holy day for you, a Sabbath day of rest to Hashem, whoever does any work on it shall be put to death.**

שבת . . .

Shabbos . . .

The word שבת, *Shabbos*, is an acronym formed of the initial letters of the phrase שינה בשבת תענוג , *sleeping on Shabbos is a delight.* This brings to mind a witty remark by Rabbi Chaim Volozhiner.

One *Shabbos* afternoon, Rabbi Chaim entered his Yeshivah to find his students engaged in trivial talk.

He gently suggested to them: "Would it not be better for you to have a nap, for as you know שבת stands for שינה בשבת תענוג, and by sleeping you would be fulfilling the *mitzvah* of *oneg Shabbos*, enjoying the *Shabbos*?

One of the students impudently replied: "The word שבת also is the acronym of שיחה בשבת תענוג, *conversing on Shabbos is considered a delight."*

Rabbi Chaim, with a twinkle in his eyes, retorted: "Shlomo Hamelech had you in mind when he said (*Koheles* 10:2) : 'The heart of a wise man is on his right, but the heart of a fool is on his left.' You see, a wise man sees the first letter of שבת as a ש, *shin*, which is punctuated on the right side, thus becoming שינה בשבת תענוג. A fool, on the other hand, interprets it as a ש, *sin*, which is punctuated on the left side, deriving the phrase שיחה בשבת תענוג."

Otzar Chaim

[לה:ג] לא תבערו אש בכל משבתיכם ביום השבת.

[35:3] **You shall kindle no fire in any of your dwellings on the Sabbath day.**

לא תבערו אש בכל משבתיכם ביום השבת

You shall kindle no fire in any of your dwellings on the Sabbath day

If we count the words in these first three verses, beginning with ויקהל until but not including the word השבת we find a total of 39 words. This number parallels the 39 *avos melachah*, the primary classifications of labors forbidden on Shabbos.

Baal Haturim

קחו מאתכם תרומה לה'...
Take from among yourselves an offering to Hashem...

The word מאתכם, *from among yourselves*, denotes an inherent personal initiative, an inner commitment to bring the offering to Hashem. The offering must come "from among and within yourselves."

There are people who will contribute to charity only after they learn that others have donated. They then follow suit, motivated by envy or by a sense of shame. Such giving cannot be characterized as מאתכם, as coming "from within yourselves." Rather, it is prompted by external forces, by the example set by others.

Kli Yakar

... כסף
... money (silver)

Rabbeinu Efraim notes that the numerical value of the word כסף, *money*, is equivalent to that of עץ, *tree*, both amounting to 160.

In the light of this *gematria*, a new meaning in the following verse emerges: עץ חיים היא למחזיקים בה, "It is a tree of life for those who grasp it." (*Mishlei* 3:18) Our Sages explained that this refers to the wealthy.

By donating their כסף, *money*, for the support of the Torah they earn a share of the עץ החיים, *Tree of Life*.

Nachal Kedumim

[לה:ה] קחו מאתכם תרומה לה' כל נדיב לבו יביאה את תרומת ה' זהב וכסף ונחשת.

[35:5] Take from among yourselves an offering to Hashem, whoever is of a willing heart shall bring it, Hashem's offering, of gold and silver and brass.

TORAH TREASURES • *Vayakheil*

[לה:כה] וכל אשה חכמת לב בידיה טוו ויביאו מטוה את התכלת ואת הארגמן את תולעת השני ואת השש.

[35:25] **And all the skilled women put their hands to spinning, and they brought the spun yarn, the blue, indigo and scarlet wool and the fine linen.**

וכל אשה חכמת לב בידיה טוו ויביאו מטוה . . .
And all the skilled women put their hands to spinning, and they brought the spun yarn . . .

This verse gives rise to an interesting question relating to the status of women.

The Halachah states that the fruit of a wife's labor belongs to her husband. This being so, how could the women offer their efforts toward the building of the *Mishkan*?

The *Gemara* (*Kesuvos* 47b) provides an answer.

The *Gemara* tells us that a wife is legally entitled to her husband's support and sustenance in exchange for her labor. In return for his support, the wife relinquishes her rights to the proceeds of her labor to her husband.

During Yisrael's sojourn in the Desert, the women were not dependent on their husbands' sustenance, since everyone received a daily ration of manna from Heaven. Consequently, the product of their handiwork accrued to them, and they were free to donate it to the *Mishkan*.

Dor Hame'ah

[לה:ל] ויאמר משה אל בני ישראל ראו קרא ה' בשם בצלאל בן אורי בן חור למטה יהודה.

[35:30] **And Moshe said to the people of Yisrael: "See, Hashem has called upon Bezalel, the son of Uri, the son of Chur, of the tribe of Yehudah."**

ראו קרא ה' בשם . . .
See, Hashem has called upon . . .

The initial letters of the words ראו קרא ה' בשם, *See, Hashem has called upon*, form the acronym יקרב, *let him draw near*.

The implication of this acronym is that Bezalel drew near to Hashem by means of his intense attachment to Torah and *mitzvos*. In return, Hashem drew Bezalel near to Himself.

This concept of reciprocity is expressed in the Rabbinic dictum: הבא לטהר מסייעין אותו, *Whoever makes a sincere effort to cleanse himself will be granted Heavenly aid.*

Chomas Anoch

ויעש בצלאל את הארן ...
And Bezalel made the ark ...

All furnishings of the *Mishkan* were reproduced for use in the first and second *Bais Hamikdash*, with the exception of the ark, which was never duplicated. The original ark of the *Mishkan* was the same one used in the first *Bais Hamikdash*.

Before the destruction of the first *Bais Hamikdash*, Yoshiah, the king at that time, hid it away to be used in the future *Bais Hamikdash*, may it be rebuilt speedily in our days. Indeed, it may be said that the ark that Bezalel built will endure forever.

This is reflected in the wording of the Torah text. When the Torah describes the ark, the phrase ויעש בצלאל, *and Bezalel made*, is used. By contrast, when discussing the other holy furnishings, it merely states ויעש, *and he made*.

Meshech Chochmah

[לז:א] ויעש בצלאל את הארן עצי שטים אמתים וחצי ארכו ואמה וחצי רחבו ואמה וחצי קמתו.

[37:1] And Bezalel made the ark of acacia wood, two cubits and a half was its length, a cubit and a half its breadth and a cubit and a half its height.

Pikudei / פקודי

אלה פקודי המשכן ...
These are the accounts of the Tabernacle ...

This verse teaches an important lesson. A treasurer of a charitable fund who single-handedly administers large sums of money is generally a person of impeccable reputation and integrity above reproach. He enjoys the complete trust of the entire community. Nevertheless, he should render a detailed accounting to the community of all his receipts and disbursements, so as to avoid even the slightest hint of impropriety.

Moshe Rabbeinu set the example for this course of action. His honesty and supreme nobility of character certainly were known to all the people of Yisrael. Nevertheless, as stated in our verse, he gave a comprehensive accounting of all the gifts that were received toward the building of the *Mishkan*, the Tabernacle.

Bais Chadash

[לח:כא] אלה פקודי המשכן משכן העדת אשר פקד על פי משה עבדת הלוים ביד איתמר בן אהרן הכהן.

[38:21] These are the accounts of the Tabernacle, the Tabernacle of the Testimony, as they were rendered according to Moshe, through the service of the Levites, by the hand of Issamar, the son of Aharon the Priest.

TORAH TREASURES • Pikudei

[לח:כא] אלה פקודי המשכן משכן העדת אשר פקד על פי משה עבדת הלוים ביד איתמר בן אהרן הכהן.

[38:21] These are the accounts of the Tabernacle, the Tabernacle of the Testimony, as they were rendered according to Moshe, through the service of the Levites, by the hand of Issamar, the son of Aharon the Priest.

אלה פקודי המשכן משכן העדת אשר פקד על פי משה ...
These are the accounts of the Tabernacle, the Tabernacle of the Testimony, as they were rendered according to Moshe ...

This verse hints at the three periods in the history of the people of Yisrael when they possessed a Sanctuary the era of the *Mishkan*, the era of the first *Bais Hamikdash* and the era of the second *Bais Hamikdash*.

The word העדת, *the Testimony*, which appears here in the abbreviated form, without a ו, *vav*, has the numerical value of 479, which corresponds to the 479 years of the existence of the *Mishkan* (from the second year after *Yetzias Mitzrayim*, the Exodus, until the building of the *Bais Hamikdash*).

The word משכן, *Tabernacle*, has a numerical value of 410, corresponding to the 410 years of the first *Bais Hamikdash*.

The word המשכן, *the Tabernacle*, has a *gematria* of 415. Add another 5 (the number of letters in the word), and we obtain a value of 420, corresponding to the 420 years of the second *Bais Hamikdash*.

The fact that the *gematria* of המשכן lacks 5 from the total of 420, which forces us to include the 5 letters, alludes to the five things that were missing in the second *Bais Hamikdash* according to the *Gemara* in *Yoma* 21b: These were the *Aron Hakodesh* (Holy Ark), the heavenly fire on the altar, the *Shechinah* (Divine Presence), *Ruach Hakodesh* (Holy Spirit of Prophecy) and the *Urim Vetumim* in the breastplate of the *Kohein Gadol* (High Priest).

Chasam Sofer

ואת האלף . . .
And of the thousand . . .

The *Midrash* tells us that when Moshe was giving the accounting for the gold, he was unable to recall how the 1775 golden shekels had been utilized. He feared that this would trigger slanderous talk of misappropriation of funds, when a Heavenly Voice called out: "And of the thousand . . . he made hooks for the pillars."

This *Midrash* prompted Rabbi Meir Shapiro to make the following cutting remark:

"Isn't it amazing? When making the golden calf the people did not demand any accounting, although they had contributed so much gold and received only one little calf. But here, even though so many impressive objects had been produced with their gold, the people were exacting to the point that Moshe needed a Heavenly Voice to silence their vicious gossip.

"Human nature is such, that when funds are collected for a golden calf, no questions are asked and everyone is satisfied, but when money is donated to holy causes, then people are skeptical and harbor misgivings."

Otzar Chaim

[לח:כח] **ואת האלף ושבע המאות וחמשה ושבעים עשה ווים לעמודים וצפה ראשיהם וחשק אתם.**

[38:28] And of the thousand seven hundred and seventy-five shekels he made hooks for the pillars and overlaid their pinnacle, and he made fillets for them.

ותכל כל עבדת משכן אהל מועד . . .
And all the work was finished on the Tabernacle of the Tent of Meeting . . .

The numerical value of ותכל כל עבדת משכן, *and all the work was finished on the Tabernacle*, is equivalent to that of בעשרים וחמשה בכסלו נגמר, *it was completed on the twenty-fifth day of Kislev* (the first day of *Chanukah*).

Baal Haturim

[לט:לב] **ותכל כל עבדת משכן אהל מועד ויעשו בני ישראל ככל אשר צוה ה' את משה כן עשו.**

[39:32] And all the work was finished on the Tabernacle of the Tent of Meeting, and the people of Yisrael did according to all that Hashem

TORAH TREASURES • *Pikudei*

[לט:לב] **ותכל כל עבדת משכן אהל מועד ויעשו בני ישראל ככל אשר צוה ה' את משה כן עשו.**

[39:32] **And all the work was finished on the Tabernacle of the Tent of Meeting, and the people of Yisrael did according to all that Hashem had commanded Moshe, so did they do.**

Author's Note:
The *Pesikta* in Chapter 6 states: Rabbi Chanina says: "On the twenty-fifth of *Kislev* the work of the *Mishkan* was completed, but he kept it folded until the first day of *Nissan*" (when Moshe Rabbeinu erected it, according to *Shemos* 40:17).

... ככל אשר צוה ה' את משה כן עשו
... according to all that Hashem had commanded Moshe, so did they do

We note that in the Torah portion of *Pikudei* each segment describing the construction of the *Mishkan*, its holy vessels and garments, concludes with the phrase "as Hashem had commanded Moshe." What possible reason could the Torah have for continually reiterating this statement?

The building of the *Mishkan* was an atonement for Yisrael's worship of the golden calf. This sinful act was rooted in their erroneous perception of the essence of Torah. Instead of serving Hashem according to the dictates of the Torah, they sought to worship Him from the perspective of their own intellect and rationale. (See commentary by *Bais Halevi* on *Terumah* 25:20 for comparison.)

When relating the construction of the *Mishkan*, which atoned for this sin, the Torah emphasizes that every minute detail was fashioned "as Hashem had commanded Moshe." In other words, even though Bezalel understood the esoteric and mystic wisdom concealed in the elements of the *Mishkan*, when executing his holy work, his sole intent was to fulfill Hashem's Will, which transcends all human bounds of logical imperative.

It was this total renunciation of self that

achieved the atonement for tne sin of the golden calf.

Bais Halevi

ויביאו את המשכן . . .
And they brought the Tabernacle . . .

[39:33] **And they brought the Tabernacle to Moshe, the Tent and all its accessories, its clasps, beams, crossbar, pillars and bases.**

[לט:לג] ויביאו את המשכן אל משה את האהל ואת כל כליו קרסיו קרשיו בריחו ועמדיו ואדניו.

The *Midrash* establishes a homiletical connection between this verse and *Mishlei* 31:25: "Strength and majesty are her attire, she joyfully awaits the last day." The *Midrash* then recounts that one day Rabbi Abahu had a vision of a higher world and was shown all the rewards in store for him in the World to Come. Elated, he exclaimed: "All this is prepared for me, and all my life I had thought I was laboring in vain!"

What is the meaning of this *Midrash*? How could Rabbi Abahu have entertained such thoughts?

A brief vignette taken from the life of the author of *Chossen Yeshuos* will help to clarify this puzzling *Midrash*.

One year, he spent *Pesach* at the home of his son, Rabbi David Meisels, a well-known intercessor with government officials on behalf of condemned Jews. Much to his sorrow, on that particular *Pesach*, he failed in an attempt to gain the release of a jailed man.

The father, noting his son's distress, gently said: "Rest assured, your reward will be complete from Hashem, as though you had actually freed the man." He continued, "This is the underlying thought of the *Midrash* concerning Rabbi Abahu. It is a known fact that Rabbi Abahu was influential at the royal court and often interceded for his fellow Jews. Of course, many times he was unsuccessful. When he was shown in his vision that he would be rewarded

TORAH TREASURES • *Pikudei*

[לט:לג] ויביאו את המשכן אל משה את האהל ואת כל כליו קרסיו קרשיו בריחו ועמדיו ואדניו.

[39:33] And they brought the Tabernacle to Moshe, the Tent and all its accessories, its clasps, beams, crossbar, pillars and bases.

even for his failed attempts he rejoiced greatly; for until that moment he had thought that only accomplishments are rewarded in Heaven."

Turning to the connenction between the *Midrash* and our verse, we can explain it in a similar vein. The craftsmen who built the *Mishkan* were dejected, for after expending so much painstaking labor, they were not permitted to complete the *Mishkan* by erecting it; they were to bring the components to Moshe who would erect it.

The *Midrash* implies that they had no reason to be dismayed, quoting "she joyfully awaits the last day." You are rewarded for good intentions though they are not brought to fruition, for good works though you do not complete them.

Devash Vechalav